To The Shore Once More

Volume II

A Journey Down The Jersey Shore ...from the tip of Sandy Hook to the point of Cape May...

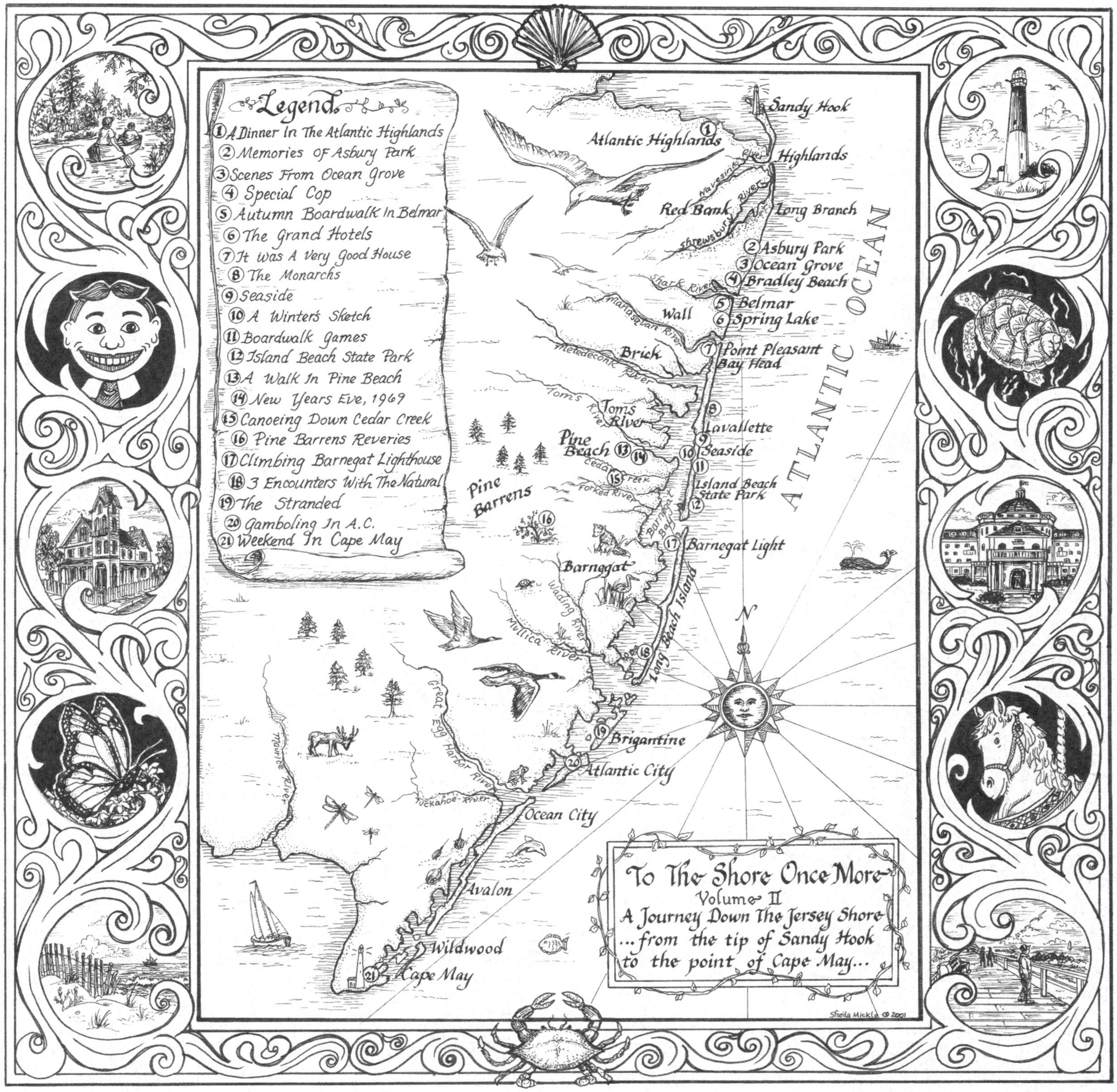

Legend

1. A Dinner In The Atlantic Highlands
2. Memories of Asbury Park
3. Scenes From Ocean Grove
4. Special Cop
5. Autumn Boardwalk In Belmar
6. The Grand Hotels
7. It Was A Very Good House
8. The Monarchs
9. Seaside
10. A Winter's Sketch
11. Boardwalk Games
12. Island Beach State Park
13. A Walk In Pine Beach
14. New Years Eve, 1969
15. Canoeing Down Cedar Creek
16. Pine Barrens Reveries
17. Climbing Barnegat Lighthouse
18. 3 Encounters With The Natural
19. The Stranded
20. Gamboling In A.C.
21. Weekend In Cape May

Sandy Hook
Atlantic Highlands
Highlands
Navesink River
Red Bank
Long Branch
Shrewsbury River
Asbury Park
Ocean Grove
Bradley Beach
Shark River
Belmar
Spring Lake
Wall
Manasquan River
Brick
Point Pleasant
Bay Head
Metedeconk River
Toms River
Pine Beach
Lavallette
Seaside
Cedar Creek
Forked River
Island Beach State Park
Pine Barrens
Barnegat Bay
Barnegat Light
Barnegat
Wading River
Mullica River
Long Beach Island
ATLANTIC OCEAN
N
Great Egg Harbor River
Maurice River
Tuckahoe River
Brigantine
Atlantic City
Ocean City
Avalon
Wildwood
Cape May

Sheila Mickle © 2001

To The Shore Once More

VOLUME II

A Journey Down The Jersey Shore

Prose, Poetry, and Works of Art

prose and poetry by
Frank Finale

works of art by
Donna Ayers • Al Barker • Alan S. Brown • Carole Clarke • Barbara J. Cocker
Carla Coutts-Miners • Symon Cowles • Kate Leigh Cutler • Cathleen P. Engelsen
Dede Esenlohr • Dennis Foy • Carol Freas • Lloyd Garrison • Beverly Golembeski
Tine Kirkland Graham • Stephen Harrington • Ann Hayes • Linda Hejduk
Dawn Hotaling • Beth Kantor • Edward J. Kojola • Paula Kolojeski • Dick LaBonté
Jane Law • Joyce Lawrence • Robert A. Loder Jr. • Susan Walsh McLean
Pauline Mickle • Sheila Mickle • Patty Niebling • Sue T. Oliver • Virginia Perle
Patricia Rainey • Greg Rogers • Muriel Rogers • Nicholas P. Santoleri
Elaine Sgambati • Ludlow Thorston • Margaret Tourison Berndt
Theresa Troise Heidel • Lea Colie Wight

foreword by editor and publisher
George C. Valente

introduction by
Rich Youmans

artwork edited by
George C. Valente and Judy Cardella

Jersey Shore Publications • Bay Head, New Jersey

Tine Kirkland Graham
"Les Trois Soeurs"
48" x 36" Acrylic 2000
Prints Available

ISBN 0-9632906-2-2
Library of Congress Catalog Number: 98-089077

Printed and bound in Hong Kong
First Edition, May 2001

The typeface used for text is Novarese Book
The paper is Shinmorrim A-2 Matt Coated, wt. 157gsm

Jersey Shore Publications
Publishers of:
To The Shore Once More (Volume I)
Jersey Shore Vacation Magazine
Jersey Shore Vacation Map
The Jersey Shore Guide Book
Jersey Shore Home & Garden

Editor and Publisher: George C. Valente
Post Office Box 176, Bay Head, New Jersey 08742-0176
Telephone: 732-892-1276 • Fax: 732-892-3365
www.jerseyshorevacation.com

For Barbara whose support made this book possible and my sons who enriched my life.

"A Winter's Night," first published in EPOS (Vol. 26, No. 3), 1976
"The Age of Faith" first published in Without Halos XI, 1994
"Alien," first published in BEYOND: Science Fiction & Fantasy (No. 3), 1986
"The Animals," first published in POEM 45, 1982
"The Beast," first published in U. S. 1 Worksheets, (Issue No. 36/37), 1997
"Flamingo: At the Cape May Zoo," first published in Sensations Magazine, (Issue 20), 2000
"Lines for Summer," first published in Green's Magazine, 1976
"Metamorphosis," first published in Without Halos V, 1987
"Release," first published in Asbury Park Press, 1982
"Retirement Village," first published in Bitterroot (Vol. XIII, No. 50), 1974
"The Shell," first published in United Poets, Summer 1968
"Survival," first published in the new renaissance (Vol. X, No. 3), 1999

Table Of Contents

Carol Freas "Blue Claw"
4 1/2" x 13" Watercolor 1999
Collection of Artist Prints Available

Donna Ayers "Rebecca Feeding Ducks"
24" x 30" Oil 1996 Private Collection

Donna Ayers "Alex And Daisey In Autumn"
32" x 34" Oil 1999 Private Collection

Works Of Art

Margaret Tourison Berndt "August Attempt"
67 1/2" x 45" Acrylic 1999 Collection of Jennifer and David Alldian Prints Available

foreword

BY GEORGE C. VALENTE

The Author

On a black and white winter's day in January, between reviewing with artist Sheila Mickle the map she was creating as a visual representation of this book and glancing out the window at hungry swans on an ice bank of the half-frozen Metedeconk River, I was finally able to see a complete vision of the new essays and poems Frank Finale had created for this book.

Looking at the legend on the map, Sheila and I discussed the sense of loss that pervades this book—the death and desolation of friends from cancer, murder, and divorce, the devastation of Asbury Park, the tearing down of old Shore landmarks like the Monmouth and Warren hotels, and the life and death struggle of animal life at the Shore, like the swans I was watching as they searched for food on a frozen river.

All show struggles and losses and the changes that come naturally with aging and the passing of time, yet Frank Finale writes about each with an affirmation and celebration of life—with prose and poetry full of love and beauty—that keeps the reader going and is at the essence of life for all of us, all in a Jersey Shore setting.

He writes of nature's changes in A *Winter's Sketch*:

"The wind howls, and the sand responds. Everything is in flux. The beach you step on today will not be the same one you step on tomorrow. But you will never know it. Nature repeats itself endlessly, ever changing, ever unchanged."

After the success of *To The Shore Once More* (*Volume* I), I asked Frank to write a second book—a sequel and companion volume to his regional bestseller. He was apprehensive about the one-year schedule but agreed. Shortly thereafter, I contacted Rich Youmans, his primary editor of the essays that appeared in Volume I (most of which had been published in COAST *Magazine*); he also agreed to work once more with his friend, and we were off and running. Thus, the writer and the editor that had created some of the most touching and profound essays about the Jersey Shore were now working together again.

There are many differences between this book and Volume I. There are four times as many artists, almost fifty percent more paintings, and more pages. The book takes place in many of the towns and regions along the coast: Frank and the artists take readers on a journey down the Jersey Shore, from the tip of Sandy Hook to the point of Cape May, through the past and present, and in all four seasons.

Many locations, landmarks, and themes appear and reappear, like the monarch butterflies fluttering throughout the stories or the spiritual connection Frank feels with the Shore and our world as written in *Canoeing Down Cedar Creek*:

"Alan and I had been out on the water now for more than two hours, and were starting to tire. We began drifting more and more, letting the current propel us. I put my hand back into the water, and for a moment imagined myself connected to the Atlantic Ocean a few miles away. I felt myself sweep past the small beaches along the creek's shore, past the white yachts in the marinas on Barnegat Bay, past the tiny Sedge Islands with their myriad wildlife, and beyond the shoals of the shifting barrier islands, into the open ocean. From the seat of this aluminum canoe, I felt as if I were connected to all the Jersey Shore—to all creation, in fact. I tilted my face toward the sun and smiled."

Once more, join acclaimed author and poet Frank Finale and his family on a journey through the past and present as he again captures life along the Shore while exploring universal themes that touch us all. I believe these graceful personal essays and poems will elicit an emotional response and lingering memory in readers for a time to come.

The Artists

The other equal element within *"To The Shore Once More, Volume II"* is the artwork—one hundred forty-four images that, when presented with the prose and poetry, create a complete vision and portrait of the Jersey Shore.

Each of the forty-one artists featured in this book is unique in style, approach, and personality. The selection of their images was made with various criteria in mind.

Our goal was not only to show the best work of the artist—which is the case in most of the images presented—but also to take into consideration the combined content of the images, as well as the concept that certain images of the Jersey Shore must be included in a book of this type. The content of the four chapters also had bearing on the selections: since the book was organized as a journey down the Shore, some works were selected for the location presented. After the selection process, if an image "worked" with an essay, we placed it nearby; however, the placement of many images was not made to go with a specific essay.

My publishing history with the artists presented is varied. Some relationships go back many years; others are newly established for this book. During recent times, readers have seen many of the images presented in this book in *Jersey Shore Vacation Magazine*, *Jersey Shore Vacation Map*, *The Jersey Shore Guide Book*, and *Jersey Shore Home & Garden*, the magazines and guide books of Jersey Shore Publications.

All of the artists are known throughout the Jersey Shore and are known regionally and nationally as well. Most of the images (originals and prints) can be seen in galleries along the Jersey Shore as well as throughout New Jersey and the United States. More about each of the artists can be found under the biographies section at the back of this book.

I believe this companion volume is one of the most enchanting and beautiful books about the Jersey Shore ever published. I hope it will bring you closer to the places you love at the Shore.

I'd like to give thanks to Frank Finale, all of the artists, Judy Cardella, Rich Youmans, Karen France, Anne Neff, Lea Colie Wight, Kellie Wood, and Marguerite Siegel.

I'd like to give special thanks to my wife, Jane, and to the Valente and Holand families, to whom my work in creating this book is dedicated.

Tine Kirkland Graham "From The Bluffs"
30" x 40" Acrylic 2000 Private Collection Prints Available

Tine Kirkland Graham "At The Pier"
18" x 24" Acrylic 2000 Prints Available

Tine Kirkland Graham "Are You Having A Good Vacation"
24" x 48" Acrylic 2000 Prints Available

Dick Labonté "Father's Arrived From The City"
18" x 24" Acrylic 1999 Collection of Mr. and Mrs. William Flounders

An Introduction To The Essays Of Frank Finale

BY RICH YOUMANS

To read these new essays by Frank Finale is to be continually inspired—and surprised. Inspired because Frank, like all true writers, has the ability to make a story come alive through the telling details. Follow him through these twenty-one essays and nineteen poems, down the one hundred twenty-seven miles of the shore's coastline, and you'll find yourself on a tour unlike any other; even long-familiar places will be seen as if for the first time. Take, for example, his description of Sandy Hook and its surrounding bay:

"The Sandy Hook peninsula looked like the profile of a dinosaur: its skull, eye, and mouth at the northernmost point, with a thick chest tapering to the legs. It even had a tail—the spit of sand connecting it to the mainland. In the distant Atlantic, I could see ships passing to and from New York Harbor, pleasure crafts of all kinds... The toy-like boats etched the bay with their small wakes, white as the stripes in the American flags that some of them flew."

Or Atlantic City:

"I begin to look for a slot that's open, taking note of the people I pass in the aisles... Everyone seems mesmerized, a feeling that's only accentuated by the many lights and mirrors that seem to pour into one another. Round light bulbs—red, yellow, green, and blue—appear everywhere, swagged from hook to hook on the ceiling. By a casino restaurant, twinkle-lights wrap around the branches of an indoor tree. Above me, neon lights rise on ascending wires and reach the high ceiling, creating a circus "Big Top" of lights. It's all very bewitching."

Or Cape May:

"Gaslight lampposts adorned the thin-as-six-o'clock walks as we ambled up one street and down another, gazing at the many pastel-colored houses. White-picket or wrought-iron fences bordered gardens of tulips, daffodils, pansies, hyacinth, and lilac. One street had a sign tacked onto an elm that swelled the sidewalk and tilted the curbing. "Caution, trees lean out into the street," it read. We were delighted to find nature being given the right of way in a town that seemed to have appeared out of time, like Brigadoon."

Through such passages, Frank not only transports readers to the Jersey Shore but deepens their experience of it, and in so doing, he will undoubtedly inspire readers to conduct their own explorations. But Frank is much more than just a tour guide *par excellence*; he is also a poet and artist. And that's where the "surprise" comes into play. A canoe trip down Cedar Creek becomes, at one point, a commentary on the intrusion of human beings into nature. A gambling trip turns into a reverie on family and love. Enter a Frank Finale essay, and you never know where you'll end up—or what emotions will be touched.

Of course, none of this comes as a shock to those familiar with Frank's previous compilation of essays and poems, *To The Shore Once More*. I had the privilege to write the introduction for that first volume as well, and in reviewing Frank's work from that collection I find that he has lost none of his gifts as a writer. Both books present equally evocative descriptions of life along the Jersey Shore, all drawn from Frank's real-life experiences—especially those involving his wife, Barbara, a constant companion in both life and literature.

Yet while this current book might be viewed as a sequel to its popular predecessor, it also differs in several important aspects. Unlike the earlier volume, which contained material that had been previously published in various magazines and anthologies, this book contains work that was written expressly for it over the course of one year. While this may have made for many exhausting nights, it also allowed Frank to plot a book that would broaden its scope of the shore. In essence, he took the entire New Jersey coastline—from Sandy Hook to Cape May—as his personal domain, exploring the notable towns and attractions that piqued his curiosity and spurred his imagination.

The book also differs from its predecessor in tone. Frank has always plumbed his experiences for material, and in the past he took moments of celebration and tenderness—family outings and holidays, for example, or romantic interludes with Barb—and depicted them as complete stories in themselves. While his new essays take similar topics, this time they've been imbued with additional dimension: taken as a whole, they show Frank in various stages of his life and, like the facets of a diamond, play off one another to enhance the overall effect. We see him as the young man, bright with innocence, and we see that innocence lost. We see him meet his future wife and her three sons, whom he soon adopts as his own, and we see them as they grow old together. We see various friends and family members, and how their sad fates—murder, divorce, terminal illness—affect those around them. In these essays, some of which are the most touching I've ever read, we see Frank trying to use his lifetime's experience to transform lost innocence into newfound wisdom.

Frank's gift is to be able to write about such moments in a way that is in itself a celebration of life. For that's what this book truly is: a celebration—of life, of the shore, and of the moments that, when totaled, make for beautiful memories. As Frank writes, *"the world could always use a little more beauty, no matter how small."* I couldn't agree more—and I'm thankful we once again have Frank Finale's essays and poems to show us how true that is.

Al Barker "Working The Surf"
10 1/2" x 22 1/2" Oil 2000 Collection of Artist Prints Available

Al Barker "Out-Going Tide"
4" x 6" Watercolor 2000

Theresa Troise Heidel "Approaching Nightfall, Spring Lake"
14 1/2" x 21 1/2" Watercolor 2000

Theresa Troise Heidel
"Spring Lake Bridge" 3 7/8" x 11 5/8"
Watercolor and Gouache 2000
Collection of John and Theresa McHugh

Theresa Troise Heidel *"Fresh From The Rain, Twin Lights"*
14" x 20" Watercolor 1996 Collection of Barbara and Edward McGloin

CHAPTER 1

Dennis Foy "GSP 106.4"
10" x 12" Oil on Board 2000 Private Collection Prints Available

Symon Cowles "Sweetly Blew The Breeze"
12" x 16" Acrylic on Wood 1999 Private Collection Prints Available

Symon Cowles "White Water"
8" x 10" Acrylic on Wood 1999 Prints Available

Lloyd Garrison "Shopping In Old Red Bank"
18" x 24" Oil 1996 Private Collection Prints Available

A Dinner In The Atlantic Highlands

We rang the bell not knowing what to expect. A trio of musical bongs echoed through the house, and then Leila answered the door. "Come in, come in," she said excitedly, hugging each of us as we stepped through the entryway. I immediately noticed the flowery kerchief wrapped around her head.

"Hope you didn't have trouble finding the place," she said. The house, an expensively appointed bi-level Tudor, was perched on the Highland hills overlooking Sandy Hook Bay, near a main road that rose to one of the highest spots in the area. Guided by Leila's directions, we had turned off that road onto a steep, stingy lane that descended for a mile or so down the hill. Wide enough for only one car, the road also had enough curves to slow me to a crawl; my foot rarely left the brake pedal the entire trip.

"We found your house fine," I said, "but I'm not used to driving such steep hills. I would hate to try it on an icy day."

"That's when we park the car and tie on skates," she said, and laughed.

The laugh did it. Even though we had not spoken to Leila in over fifteen years, ever since she and my brother had divorced, I would have recognized that laugh anywhere—it seemed to burst from her body, like some winged creature, full of joy and life—and, hearing it, I was thankful we were here. But then, Leila had always had a special place in my life. It was she who had encouraged me to come down to Point Pleasant and live there after I graduated college. "The superintendent is a good friend of mine," she had told me. "I'm sure if I ask him, he can get you a job." She had been on friendly terms with a lot of important people back then: the police chief, the judge, the editor of the local newspaper. Even though she had only an eighth-grade education, each of these people had found something special in her. Perhaps it was her being brought up in a Jamaican orphanage and making it out of there and into the "good life": a new car, a house, four kids, a respectable husband. Maybe it was her mysterious side—she gave Tarot card readings and had psychic premonitions about events that often came to pass. Perhaps it was because she was an attractive young woman at the time: well-built, dark skin and eyes, shiny black hair, vivacious.

Or maybe it was the way she truly cared about people and was always willing to help them. This aspect of her I had the fortune to find out about first hand. When I bought my first used car, it was Leila who took the time to teach me how to drive it on the backroads of Point Pleasant. She also helped me to find a winter rental when I first moved to the shore, and invited me over to supper at least once a week. She would pick me up from school and take me to their home, where my young nieces and I would make a ritual of watching that Gothic TV comedy *The Addams Family*, snapping our fingers to the catchy theme song about the totally weird but lovable characters.

But what had endeared Leila to me most was how, years later, when Barb and I finally decided to get married, she arranged to have our wedding ceremony at her home in West Long Branch. I told her we were thinking of having it on the beach at sunrise, but Leila insisted: she would take care of everything.

For the occasion, she created a beautiful white trellis in her home and entwined daisies, golden asters, and some yellow roses around it. She put out a lovely buffet of scrambled eggs, omelets, pancakes, bacon, sausages, ham, jellies, jams, a variety of breads, and fresh fruits. She asked my cousin, who performs professionally, to play his guitar and sing *The Wedding Song*. She hired the mayor of West Long Branch to marry us. She arranged to make sure that someone would take photographs of it all. She had her girls decorate our car with a "Just Married" sign and attach a string of cans and crepe paper. It was a beautiful day, and at the end of it our twenty-five guests showered us with handfuls of rice as we drove off, rattling and clanking, toward the Poconos, white grain still peeking from our hair.

But that had been long ago, in happier times—before the pressures of maintaining that "good life" had driven Leila and my brother apart. He began working longer hours, then started a relationship with an office co-worker. She began spending more and more time traveling back to her native Jamaica, as my nieces grew up and moved out to their various private schools and colleges. By the time the divorce became final, it was a formality. Leila and I made a few attempts to stay in touch, but then our individual lives swept us away and we lost contact.

And we would still have been lost to each other, if my brother had not suffered a fatal heart attack. At the funeral, one of my nieces, Mary, told me that her mother had been given only a few months to live: she had a brain tumor that was inoperable and was being treated with chemotherapy. "I'm sure she would like to see both of you again," Mary said to us.

In fact, Leila did seem happy to see us—her eyes shone as brightly as her smile, and her face radiated joy. And I felt the same; it was as if a decade and a half had never passed, and we had seen each other only last week. But there was also a shadow in the midst of all this lightness, and I couldn't ignore it. I wondered whether I should ask about her cancer, and if so, how. True to form, Leila dispelled all unease with a simple gesture. Sliding away the kerchief, she pointed to her beautifully round and smooth bald head. Since she was only five feet tall, her head radiated whatever light shone on it. With her

Dawn Hotaling "Summer Shade"
16" x 23" Watercolor 1991 Collection of Artist Prints Available

large, dark eyes and complexion, she gave off a strange, child-like aura even though she was in her mid-sixties.

"So what do you think?" she said. "Can I get a part in the next *Star Trek* movie?"

I couldn't help it; I burst out laughing. "Leila, you are beautiful," I said, and truly meant it.

"I bet you say that to all the bald girls," she laughed with a wink.

She then told us how the cancer had first appeared a little over two years before, and the doctors had given her only a couple of months to live. After the first year passed, she thought she had beaten it.

"But now it's back," she said. "The chemotherapy helps a bit, but afterward I can't do anything for a couple of days. Fortunately, today I'm feeling fine."

"Leila, your head is so beautiful, why do you wear a kerchief?" Barb asked. "You have nothing to be ashamed of."

"You're right, I don't," Leila said, smiling. "But I *do* like to keep it warm."

She bustled into the kitchen to check on the roast ribs and yams she was preparing, then returned and motioned us back toward the door. "Come outside, I'll show you my garden," she said. Leila had always been proud of her gardens; when she lived in Point Pleasant, she would spend hours tending to her plants, as if each were one of her children.

Outside, adjacent to the house, a small woodland setting had been terraced into the hillside. In the twilight, I spotted moss and impatiens. In a descending fountain, water flowed from one concrete bowl to another larger one below it, finally emptying into a circular pool adorned with cherubs and surrounded by pansies and white, yellow, and red tulips. Next to it stood a three-foot statue of St. Jude, the patron saint of lost causes and Leila's favorite.

"It's wonderful," I said. I spotted wild strawberries running up the side of the slope. "I bet you keep plenty of shortcake handy."

Leila noticed where I was looking. "Same old Frank," she said. "Always thinking with his stomach."

We went back inside to the dining room, the showcase of the house. Sliding glass doors led us onto a redwood deck overlooking a steep incline of woods and a few rooftops. Beyond them, the Sandy Hook peninsula looked like the profile of a dinosaur: its skull, eye, and mouth at the northernmost point, with a thick chest tapering to the legs. It even had a tail—the spit of sand connecting it to the mainland. In the distant Atlantic, I could see ships passing to and from New York Harbor, pleasure crafts of all kinds, and the commuter ferry that left Red Bank and went to New York twice a day. The toy-like boats etched the bay with their small wakes, white as the stripes in the American flags that some of them flew.

"It's an awesome view," I said. "I could spend hours out here gazing down and watching the ebb and flow of life."

"Or gazing up," Leila said. "Remember, we're also under the Atlantic Flyway, and it's not unusual to see a chevron of geese or a lone heron or pelican in full flight."

We returned to the living room, and for a while we caught up on the past fifteen years. After the divorce, Leila had married an older man who, as she put it, "treated her like a princess." He had passed away a few years before, but they had at least managed to celebrate their tenth wedding anniversary.

"Barb and I have been married for nearly thirty years now—but you know that," I laughed, "having been the one who almost single-handedly made sure we had a wedding."

Leila smiled. "That was a good time," she said. "I'm always impressed when couples can stay happy together for that

Lea Colie Wight "Beach Cousins"
24" x 36" Oil 2000

Lea Colie Wight "Beach Day"
18" x 24" Oil 2000

long. I think sometimes a little trickery must be necessary. Remember when your parents stayed with us briefly? Your mother was always asking your dad to do some chore or another, so sometimes I would give him a newspaper and a beer, put him in the garage where it was cooler, and lock the garage door. Your mother would go around the house asking, 'Where did that guy go to now?' and I'd just tell her not to worry, that dad was helping me to clean the garage."

I laughed. "Yeah, mom could get like that, but dad would just ignore her. Maybe you're right, good marriages do need a little trickery—or a little magic," I said, looking at Barb.

"Well, it's all in the past now," Leila said wistfully, and for a moment some sadness came into her eyes. But then she cheered again. "Frank, do you remember when you would come over to watch *The Addams Family*..."

And so it went, memories and laughter swirling around us until the timer went off in the kitchen. "Time to eat," Leila said. "You two sit at the table, and I'll begin bringing in the food."

We did so, and when Leila came back with a pan of roasted prime ribs and took off the lid, the steam billowed up and filled the room with its savory aroma. The cuts were large, juicy, tender, and still on the bone. Next came the dishes of candied yams, baked potatoes, Jersey corn on the cob, and hot muffins. Beverages included wine, soda, and a sweating pitcher of iced tea. Dessert, Leila informed us, would be homemade peanut butter cookies and ice cream. "So leave room," she instructed.

It was amazing, I thought to myself. Here's this woman who was near death, and she still had the desire and energy to prepare a meal for ex-relatives she hadn't seen in fifteen years. But then, she was always tough. Once, her car was hit by a freight train: one of her young ones had accidentally knocked the gear stick and popped it into forward. The front end of the station wagon was demolished, and all fifty train cars had passed before she could climb out and get help. Fortunately, she and the children were fine, and the next week, she was driving again.

"I thank St. Jude," she told me afterward. "When you think things are hopeless, you should pray to him." She had always thanked St. Jude for any good thing that occurred.

Not surprisingly, the meal was delicious. Afterward, Barb and I helped clean off the table, and Leila made coffee. When I asked her if she still did readings, she immediately brought out her Tarot cards, which were wrapped in a red and gold paisley print velvet cloth surrounded by fringes. I shuffled the cards until they felt right and gave them back to her. Leila then laid them out and proceeded to tell my fortune. Although I always took the predictions with a grain of salt, I enjoyed listening to them.

"I see you having many grandchildren and writing a successful book," she said. Then, as an afterthought, she told me our current house would not be the last. The predictions brought back memories of when she was a young woman and gave readings at her kitchen table in Point Pleasant. There was a tense thrill to these readings, just as in gambling. What would turn up next? Would it be a win or a loss? If it were a loss, you wanted an immediate win afterward: one card might show your house burning down, but the next card would show the people in the community rallying around you and helping you to get a better one. I wondered if Leila ever did readings for herself. I didn't ask.

By this time, both Barb and I could see that Leila was getting tired. As we prepared to leave, I asked Leila if she wouldn't mind my going out on the deck one more time.

"I knew you would like that deck," Leila said, perking up.

"Go right ahead."

Outside, the air had turned chill—a sign of the coming fall and winter. Seasons turn, cycles of life change, and all we can do is try to capture as many good moments as we can—and remember. I put both hands on the deck's grainy wooden railing and looked out toward the New York skyline, which by now was an abstract design of lights. Faintly, I could see the lights of the Verrazano Narrows Bridge, a web spangled with beads of dew. And, over the ocean and light years away, those natural fires that consume themselves in space gleamed, giving us but a glimmer of their energy. "Goodbye, Leila," I said, quietly.

Two months later, Leila slipped away peacefully in her oldest daughter's arms. I like to think that she was pretty close to the heavens in that house, and didn't have far to go to reach those stars.

Kate Leigh Cutler "Moonlit Dory"
18" x 24" Watercolor 2000
Private Collection Prints Available

Carla Coutts-Miners "Best Fishes"
14" x 11" Watercolor and Gouache 1999 Collection of C. Andrew Coutts Prints Available

Alien

We are star beings
pieces and bits of God
and the sun itself.

Shot into the seas
and cooled, we emerged
our hearts still

hot with genesis
of sun's forge and the God
that hammered us

into this blue planet
where air and water
feed and calm our fire.

We are star beings
half light, half
dark, we turn—

the hammer trips in our hearts
the tongues of flame still
in our brain.

Lights in the water
reflect and shimmer
our names.

The Age Of Faith

At night these houses are lighted ships,
sails of curtains flying from second story
windows as they hold their cargo
of families under steep hands-of-prayer
roofs, silently above a highway
of lamplights and below a ream of stars.
So many possibilities bud and leaf
under the wooden roofs and beanstalk moon:
a Jack grows up to be a giant-killer;
a Jill becomes a surgeon; Hansel
and Gretel turn jewelers. On the highway
below them, headlights follow
three glowing trails into the night.

Survival

Caught in maple   a plastic bag
        outlasts snows, leaves & all who
                pass beneath—
never blooms in spring or
        colors in fall.
Its shadow appears shaking
        on snow—some frantic buck
its antlers caught in the branches. One grows
        attached to such
Absaloms of nature—grows
        somehow in the Angelus
of seeing them. Such odd devotion
        raises the eyes
        to see
        what is
in the tree. And
        what is not.

Theresa Troise Heidel "The Swan, Asbury Park"
30" x 40" Watercolor and Gouache 1995 Collection of Dr. and Mrs. Howard Silver Prints Available

Robert A. Loder Jr. "Palace Amusements, Asbury Park"
11" x 14" Acrylic 1995 Prints Available

Memories Of Asbury Park

The first time I saw Asbury Park was in the spring of 1965. Having moved from Brooklyn to Point Pleasant at the age of twenty-two, I was searching for a place that had some of the excitement I was used to in the old borough: movie houses, their marquees flashing the latest Hollywood stars, or nightclubs from which the familiar beats of rock tunes flowed as patrons entered; a potpourri of people chatting and laughing, calling to each other from second-story apartment windows, or harmonizing on street corners. Brooklyn vibrated with colors, lights, and sounds, whereas Point Pleasant seemed to undergo a blackout every evening in the off-season, with shops closed tight, sidewalks empty, and area nightclubs few.

When I asked a local one afternoon where I could find some action, he suggested two places: Seaside Heights, which was located just a few miles south, and Asbury Park. "But Asbury Park is better. It's open all year 'round on the weekends," he said, a wild smile crossing his face. I needed no further convincing, and set out in my "new" car—a '55 Chevy Bel Air with cream-colored top, blue-green body, and white interior. For reasons that mystified the garage mechanics, the car destined to become a classic did not start well in the rain and stalled out consistently near the tops of high bridges. But I didn't care: neither problem threatened that afternoon, as I set out on what would be until then the longest trip I had ever taken in the Bel Air. I didn't quite know where I was going, except that Asbury Park was due north and one of the main train stops along the coast. After about thirty-five minutes—during which time I had to ask directions only once—I found it.

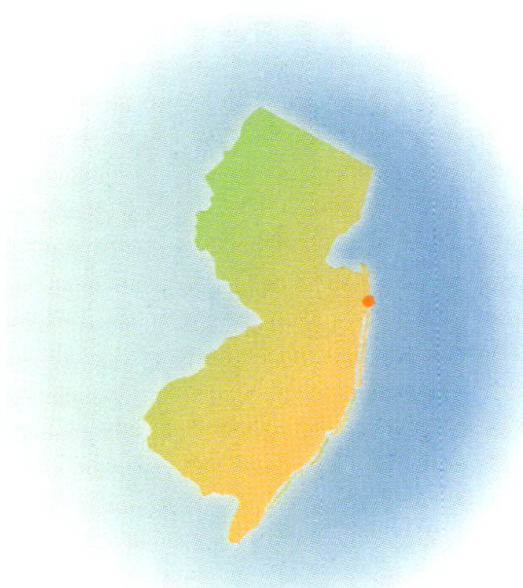

I'm not sure what I had expected, but I was surprised to see a crowded town with office buildings and hotels that were several stories tall, and a downtown business district where shoppers walked hurriedly from store to store, bundled with packages. The flagship department store, Steinbachs, rose three stories and took up an entire triangle-shaped block. Making a right turn off Main Street, I drove wide-eyed down Lake Avenue, on the right side of which Wesley Lake glittered in the midday sun. Farther down, on the corner of Lake and Saint James, I came across the Mayfair, a gigantic movie theater that dominated the avenues. Unlike any theater I had ever seen, it had Spanish stucco, Baroque columns, a tall balconade, and a bell tower that rose high above the lake.

This was more like it, I thought, the boredom of Point Pleasant fading away as I drove. To my delight, I discovered next to the theater a bit of Coney Island's atmosphere in the form of the Palace Amusements; the arcade took up a whole block and had bumper cars, a Tunnel of Love, a carousel, a fun house (which you entered through an actual rolling barrel), a mechanical gypsy fortune teller, and pinball games galore. Farther down, a Ferris wheel as high as the bell tower turned slowly, its riders facing the lake where a giant swan boat glided serenely. A couple of pedal boats built for two followed like small cygnets.

Near the end of the surreal avenue, a circular glass carousel house spun into view, its arched windows decorated by screaming, Medusa-like faces. Inside, brightly painted ponies pranced up and down and around and around to the organ music. I was tempted to stop, but instead followed Lake Avenue as it curved left into an especially wide thoroughfare—Ocean Avenue. If Lake had been active, Ocean seemed frenetic. Within a few blocks, I counted numerous nightclubs: The Stone Pony, Mrs. Jay's, the African Room, the Student Prince, all within walking distance of one another. Across from them, running parallel to the avenue, lay the teeming boardwalk. At the south end, lights bounced and flashed at the Casino pier, which I eventually discovered had an indoor skating rink. Farther down, a roller coaster roared under sweeping gulls, and windmills rose from miniature golf courses. Up and down the boardwalk, I noted the many booths that could satisfy my taste for sweets—hand-dipped chocolates, salt-water taffy made on site, cotton candy, frozen custard, lemonade, and ices. I spotted the kiosk-like booth of Madame Marie, the gypsy fortune teller; there, painted on a whitewash background, a big eye stared back at me, surrounded by a ringed planet and the words "Temple of Knowledge." At the north end stood the Paramount Theater and Convention Hall, and, across from them, the imperious Berkeley-Carteret Hotel. The Paramount, I later learned, featured large rock concerts with bands such as the Doors, the Rolling Stones, and the Who, and Judy Garland had once stayed in one of the Berkeley-Carteret's two hundred fifty-four rooms.

Turning at the hotel and traveling south on Kingsley, I spotted the icon of Asbury Park: the oval face and crazy, toothy smile of Tilly, a little imp made bright with neon lights on the wall of the Palace Amusements. His dark hair was parted in the middle and slightly turned up on each side like two little horns. Reminding me of the zany face at the Steeplechase Park in Coney Island, he made me feel a little more at home in my new state.

That first ride of the circuit was one of many I would take in the months to come. I began going to the Mayfair Theater, where Spanish stucco was hand-sculpted, the ornate campanile (whose chimes no longer worked) rose one hundred seventy-two feet high, and the auditorium seated two thousand. It was one of the most ornate theaters I had ever seen, with its marble stairs, crystal chandeliers and crushed velvet carpeting in the lobby, and its uniformed ushers who would lead me to my seat. The first time I went up the magnificent, curved marble staircase and onto the large balcony, I stared in

Theresa Troise Heidel "Convention Hall, Asbury Park"
25" x 40" Watercolor 1992 Collection of Dr. and Mrs. Howard Silver

Theresa Troise Heidel

"Sea Serpents, Convention Hall, Asbury Park"
11" x 15" Watercolor 2000

"Winged Seahorse, Convention Hall"
11" x 15" Watercolor 2000

"Convention Hall Detail"
15" x 10" Watercolor 1994
Collection of Donald and Joan Norkus

wonder at the ceiling's nighttime "sky," complete with twinkling stars and an occasional cloud. Because of its wide CinemaScope screen, a novelty back then, the theater showed many re-released, visually stunning movies, such as *Ben-Hur* and *The Ten Commandments*.

After the movie, I would often go to the Student Prince and listen to Joe Finn, an Irish folksinger who played guitar. A number of the songs he sang were sing-alongs, and he always ended the night with a rousing, "*I don't wanna go home / I don't wanna go home / I'm having too much fun / Send the bartenders home / Send the ladies home / But save me just one*." I met an actor-writer there who said he was writing a novel about the Jersey Shore that he would title *I Don't Wannna Go Home*. I couldn't have agreed more.

It was there in October that I also met a woman I first spotted singing along to Finn's songs, her long red hair bouncing to the music. When the song ended, she stood up and turned around. She was tall, curvy, and had a bright smile. During a break in the set, I sauntered over, introduced myself, and asked if I could join her. Her name was Barbara, and she had a clear, bell-like voice and green-brown eyes with gold flecks. After talking for a while, trading information about places to go and things to do, I asked her for a date. I told her that I wasn't interested in getting married or having children. She laughed and said, "I'm not interested in getting married, either, but I have three children from a previous marriage." I gulped, but we agreed to meet for dinner.

That first date led to others, and over time we discovered things in each other that we liked and didn't want to throw away. I admired her calm, take-charge attitude when other people normally panicked. One time, while we were passing a boarding house on the way home from a date, she spotted smoke. Without hesitating, she grabbed my arm and told me to tell the people in the next house to call the fire department. As I did, she ran into the boarding house and began knocking on doors, alerting the boarders and helping them out. I also liked the way she cared and went out of her way for other people, as she did for the young waitress that needed a place to live after leaving an abusive husband: Barb put her up for a couple of days and helped her secure a room of her own. Our song became *We'll Sing In The Sunshine*. I moved to Asbury to be closer to her.

That summer, when not with Barb, I wrote by Sunset Lake (the second of the town's three magnificent lakes, the last being Deal) or walked up and down the boardwalk. But most of my time was spent with her. In July, she and I took her three children to see the fireworks. Asbury always put on the biggest and best display of all the surrounding towns: it lasted for half an hour or more and crescendoed with a finale lasting three or four minutes. The boardwalk shook as if in the middle of a tremendous thunderstorm, and the pungent smell of powder, smoke, and, for some reason, damp newspapers filled the salt air. The two older boys—Michael, four, and Alan, two—enjoyed them, but one-year-old Steven only cried, "Loud!"

When fall came and the leaves turned colors, Barb and I decided to continue our relationship. That Christmas, I gave her money to buy gifts for the children and a small tree for the apartment. When spring bloomed, we were still together. We went up to the boardwalk dressed in our best to watch the Easter parade: the ladies in hats and gloves, matching shoes and bags; the men in suits with red roses in their lapels; the babies in their bonnets. Not too long after that, we married and moved away from Asbury to Bradley Beach and a bigger apartment.

Throughout the next thirty-plus years, Barb and I weathered the shoals of life—illnesses, lack of money, family crises,

Alan S. Brown "Asbury Park Carousel"
48" x 60" Oil 1990 Collection of Dr. Walter and Omega Ashby

deaths. The same could not be said of Asbury Park. Its decline began with the race riots that erupted in the early seventies, around the same time that many of the downtown stores began migrating into the emerging malls; when Steinbachs finally left in the late seventies, it took the heart of the district with it. Fewer visitors arrived every year, and more residents moved away. In the late eighties, the Palace Amusements closed, and plans for reviving the oceanfront sank when the developers went bankrupt. Hope seemed to have run out.

Recently, Barb and I visited Asbury for the first time in many years, and were saddened by what we found. Pigeons had taken over the old Steinbachs building, now boarded up and crumbling. Where the Mayfair Theater once rose over the lake, there was an empty lot with rubble. The Palace Amusements building had been deemed structurally unsound and cordoned off; paint peeled off Tilly's face and manic smile, and his neon lights swung in the wind. The Ferris wheel had been taken apart and sold. The circular glass-and-brass carousel house remained, but the hand-painted wooden ponies were gone, replaced by a skating rink.

Along Ocean Avenue, the skeleton of a ten-story, half-finished condominium rusted in the ocean breeze, cutting off two lanes on the left side of the avenue; it had become the unofficial symbol of the derelict city. The Stone Pony, where Bruce Springsteen had gotten his start and revisits every so often, was still there, though under a new manager who is attempting to restore the famous club to its glory days. Our favorite spot, the Student Prince, had been turned into a go-go bar, with a male counterpart, Zippers, on the corner nearby. The day we visited, a disheveled man with a gray beard sat with his back against the wall, his legs sprawled across the sidewalk and his head tossed back. He was drinking from a bottle in a brown paper bag.

Fortunately, not everything proved to be so bleak. The Paramount Theater still featured concerts and plays, and Convention Hall—a huge brick building with lanterns and flying seahorse decorations—continued to host boat shows, wrestling matches, and rock concerts; Bruce Springsteen and the reunited E-Street Band had used it to rehearse for one of his U.S. tours. The red-brick Berkeley-Carteret, restored in 1991 with four spoke-like buildings surrounding a central tower, reminded me of what Asbury had been, and could be. Farther down, Madame Marie's Temple of Knowledge still stood, its all-knowing eye staring out blindly.

Everything that dies has a way of coming back; Springsteen sang it, and I've seen it for a fact. That day, I wondered if Asbury would ever return to its former self. Walking along Ocean Avenue, I found the possibility hard to believe. It was high summer, noon, and no one walked the streets. The few shops that remained operative had their corrugated metal doors and windows rolled down. An old newspaper tumbled across the deserted avenue and into the empty parking spaces. They were all empty.

Despite this, I couldn't help but hope that Asbury, the once lively city where Barb and I had met, would someday rise from its own ashes. I turned up onto the near-deserted boardwalk, where only an old woman sat mumbling to herself and occasionally laughing out loud. Staring out over the wide expanse of beach, I thought of the nights thirty years ago when I first walked these boards, the crowds thick and the neon hot under the summer stars. I thought of the first time I met Barb, her bell-like voice echoing Joe Finn's lyrics, her laugh sounding a perfect note. I thought of the city's beautiful lakes, and their adjacent parks. I thought of the restored Berkeley-Carteret, the Paramount, and Convention Hall. I thought of all the changes and the possibilities, and for a moment I was glad to be in this wild city by the great Atlantic, where the tide rolls in twice a day, through hard times and good.

Release

When I heard that train
all steam, steel and bells
whistle down the gleams,
I stood entranced by
film-framed windows flicking
till the end dwindled
down the rails—the last show's dot.
Back to the house on my own
steam, huffing shapes
in the night. It was
Friday—payday—and
anything could happen.

Ringing A Bell

I was terrified when I first met you.
In this photo, you are twenty-three.
You hold a six-month-old child.
You wear a red hairband. The background
curtains hide a closet of Salvation
Army clothes. Outside the frame of the photo
two more children, ages one and three,
wait for their macaroni and cheese. One
bangs his highchair with a spoon. The other
whines, "Is it ready?" Your husband
left last month. Still, you paused a moment
with child to have this photo taken.
You told me about Maine and how
you were really destitute then. You lived
in a condemned building and had to put
bells around the baby's crib for fear
of rats. I, fresh out of college,
could not afford your poverty. Our song
became "We'll Sing In The Sunshine."

The children, grown and gone, now have children
of their own. We vacation in Cape May.
After breakfast, we walk the beach. You pause,
gaze out at the sea and remember the rat-
jingling days of your youth. Smiling
white as the breakers, you step over
the splintered shells of the tideline
and wade into the shine of the sea.

Theresa Troise Heidel "North End Hotel, The Archway, Ocean Grove"
26 1/2" x 38" Watercolor 2000

Scenes From Ocean Grove

One Sunday back in the late 1960s, while driving along Route 71 from Bradley Beach to Asbury Park, I first came upon the anachronism called Ocean Grove. Driving past the town's main entrance—two sturdy brick pillars that braced the road—I found all access had been barred by a heavy, padlocked chain that stretched from pillar to pillar. "Wow," I thought. "What event is going on *there*?" At least a dozen cars had been stranded at the entryway, but I could see no sign or notice explaining why.

I later learned that, for residents of Ocean Grove, the Sabbath was a day to be observed peacefully and quietly—which meant no wheeled vehicles were permitted in view. In fact, the town's narrow streets really weren't built for cars, which seemed especially strange in the car-culture state of New Jersey. But then, that was Ocean Grove—or "Ocean Grave," as so many called the town because of its policies. Traffic and almost every amusement—swimming, boating, the reading of newspapers—were banned on Sundays, and liquor was forbidden every day of the week. It had been that way since the town's first camp meeting in 1870, back when a group of Methodists decided to promote a retreat at the seashore where Christians could come together for prayer meetings, preaching, and the tonic of the sea, "free from the temptations of dissipation."

This went on for over a hundred years. Finally, in 1980, after a court ruled that a conflict between church and state existed, the gates opened on Sunday. Most of the restrictions were relaxed, and cars came and went every day of the week. Still, the only spirits permitted were those of a holy nature invoked by the many noted preachers—Billy Sunday, Norman Vincent Peale, Billy Graham, and others—that came to speak at the town's Great Auditorium.

Built in 1894, the solid-wood Auditorium has long been the soul of Ocean Grove. The largest building of its kind devoted to evangelical Christianity, it seats over seven thousand people and takes up its own block at the center of the town. Its exterior is painted a light, creamy tan with green trim, and its architecture is Victorian, complete with turrets and cupolas. Three conical towers rise from the roof, the tallest of which is centrally positioned and recessed. From the middle tower, an eighteen-foot white cross radiates sunlight. Make no mistake, this is a Christian town.

Yet this is also a town that enjoys entertainment. On Sundays, the Auditorium features the Worship and Entertainment Series. Dionne Warwick, the Irish Rovers, the Drifters, and the Platters have been just a few of the acts that have performed here. For the Worship portion of the bill, undoubtedly the Auditorium's massive pipe organ comes into play. (My wife's high school graduation ceremony took place in the Auditorium, and she said you could hear the organ playing the Processional for blocks around.)

Surrounding this motherly structure, like a group of small children, are the playful tents where those "pilgrims" seeking the tonic of the sea stayed. All privately owned, these tents still come to life during the summer with their striped awnings and carnival of colors: blues, whites, yellows, reds, and greens. Their tiny wooden porches usually have one or two rockers, as well as a few plants and miniature flower boxes. Elfin white picket fences and small green hedges border the fronts of many of them. The year could be 1900, by these tents, if it were not for people's style of dress.

In the green rectangle of a park next to the Great Auditorium, I sit on one of the benches. Many pigeons walk and fly about. Under the umbrella of a mottled sycamore, I pause and think about Mrs. Crook, my wife's "adopted" grandmother and a good friend to the both of us. In the late 1960s, she lived on one of the nearby streets with her poodle in a tiny cottage. She was an artist and in her sixties, but she still wore the styles of the day—a miniskirt and go-go boots—and looked good in them, an independent woman. Barb and I were in our twenties, and when we visited, Mrs. Crook would tell us that she was worried about her teenage granddaughter, who had run away to go to some big music festival in upstate New York. Did we know anything about the festival? We tried to console her worries and tell her that it's probably a once-in-a-lifetime thing and that she would come back. The year was 1969, the festival was Woodstock; the world impinging on Ocean Grove. The granddaughter did come back, and it was a once-in-a-lifetime happening. Mrs. Crook was grateful and gave us the painting that Barb admired of the morning glories that grew in front of the cottage. It hangs in our home still to remind us of Mrs. Crook and her tiny cottage in Ocean Grove, the quaint, quiet town in which she loved to paint and worship.

From the Auditorium to the ocean runs an esplanade of about two or three short blocks, with several lawns dissected by pavement. The lawns blaze green on bright days, and the incense of mown grass permeates the hot air and intoxicates the senses to a point where you can feel guiltily high in this dry town. Walk down to the ocean, and you can see Ocean Grove was well planned; the houses nearest the ocean are

Paula Kolojeski "Beach Scene"
12" x 18" Pastel 2000 Private Collection Prints Available

built back from the street a little, so as to funnel the sea breeze westward and allow more porches farther down the street to enjoy the ocean view.

Ocean Grove lies between the once-thriving resort town of Asbury Park to the north and the family, residential town of Bradley Beach on the south side. All three towns have a boardwalk. At the northern end of Ocean Grove's boardwalk, I can see Asbury Park's formerly elegant Casino, once used as a roller rink. Its two four-story columns, one on each side of the main entrance, are still topped by large sea lanterns. A flying seahorse remains attached to the left column, hovering still, but its companion on the right column has flown, leaving only a jagged edge where it used to be. The many windows are mostly broken, and vegetation, vines, and pigeons have taken over the inside of the hollow-eyed building. It is ironic that Ocean Grove's wooden Auditorium, built in 1894, is still in use, while the much younger concrete-and-steel Casino—one of the symbols of Asbury Park's glory days—has gone to rack and ruin.

Along the Ocean Grove boardwalk, there are only two commercial establishments—a store selling towels and beach-related attire, and a white and blue-trim restaurant that extends onto the beach. Instead, the boardwalk is dominated by wide, wooden buckets with pansies, petunias, geraniums, and other plants. They have been placed among the lamp-posts and benches that have small metal plaques reading "In Loving Memory of..." or "Donated by..." Many of the benches face the beach and ocean; a few face the wide avenue and the row of four- and five-story buildings with gingerbread trim, columned porches, cupolas, turrets, awnings, and names like House by the Sea, Spray View, Silversands, and the Ocean Pride. An elderly woman with a straw broom sweeps the sidewalk in front of her home. Ocean Grove has one of the largest concentrations of Victorian houses outside of Cape May, and it also has the honor of being designated a National Historic District. It's a far cry from the surrounding towns, where people fight against the odds to save a few meager pieces of their town's history in landmarks and old buildings. In Ocean Grove, such preservation has become a way of life.

About halfway down the boardwalk is the pavilion for the Ocean Grove Summer Band and Gospel Musical Ministries. Under its roof, long benches run before a slightly raised stage, with the beach, ocean, and sky serving as a backdrop. On one of the benches, a dove with a string of beach grass in its beak alights and waits a few seconds, then flutters up to a roof beam. There, another, smaller dove is nesting by the mesh wiring on a rusted steel girder. She takes the grass and places it in the nest. He leaves and soon returns with another piece. Their gentle cooing is the only music heard in the pavilion today. A smell of freshly cut grass mixes with the salt air.

I walk over and look up at the nesting doves. The smaller one looks down at me and coos. They seem to have found their place on this earth, here in the beams of an oceanside pavilion. I wish them luck and hope their nest will not be disturbed—although that is unlikely, given where they built it. But then I think of how the original Methodists who came to Ocean Grove, attracted by two shining lakes and an ocean, were blessed in discovering their place in the sun, and how they transformed it into a sanctuary that withstood the test of time. Perhaps the doves have a chance after all. "Peace to you," I say to them, and to all those seeking sanctuary in this town where faith lives on.

Theresa Troise Heidel "Sunlit Tents, Ocean Grove"
9" x 13" Watercolor 2000 Collection of Regina Courtney

Theresa Troise Heidel

"Tent In Dappled Sunlight"
11 1/4" x 14" Watercolor 1999
Collection of Lenore Curti

"Tents, Ocean Grove, NJ"
10" x 14" Watercolor 1992
Collection of Mr. and Mrs. Kurt Spero

Paula Kolojeski "Bradley Beach"
16" x 24" Pastel 1994 Private Collection Prints Available

Special Cop

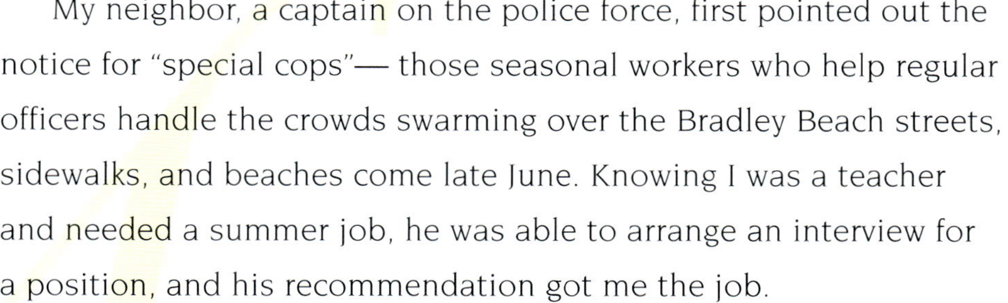

My neighbor, a captain on the police force, first pointed out the notice for "special cops"— those seasonal workers who help regular officers handle the crowds swarming over the Bradley Beach streets, sidewalks, and beaches come late June. Knowing I was a teacher and needed a summer job, he was able to arrange an interview for a position, and his recommendation got me the job.

"Don't worry," he said, noting my apprehension over carrying a gun for the first time in my life. "Don't try to be a hero, and you'll be fine."

My apprehension soon gave way to excitement, as training began in the town's recreation hall. Our instructor was a young officer named Jack. A graduate of the Sea Girt Police Academy, Jack was up and coming on the small-town police force. A homegrown boy who had been a swimming star at the local high school, he was well liked and admired by the town's people. He knew what he was doing: local policework, he said, would be his life.

In that recreation hall, Jack instructed me in the basics of law enforcement. "Never draw your weapon unless your life depends on it, or you catch an arsonist in the act," he warned. "And when you stop a vehicle, always approach from the rear. Tell the driver to stay in the car. You never know what you're dealing with. Ten years ago, an officer from this town died, shotgunned down on a routine traffic check. Remember: no traffic check is ever routine."

Spurred on by such dire stories, I paid special attention when Jack taught us how to shoot. It wasn't as easy as it seemed on TV, where cops hit their targets while somersaulting over packing crates or car hoods; no Lone Ranger stuff here. The gun seemed to weigh twenty pounds, and every shot exploded with a kick I could barely control. We fired at the silhouettes of potential assailants, our shots popping like a string of firecrackers, until my hand and forearm began to ache.

I had more misses than hits, and I began to worry about what would happen on the street.

Jack calmed me down. My first time in uniform, I had no hat that fit. Jack told me to stop by his place, a small second-floor apartment over a grocery; he had extras.

"Look," he told me as he handed me a medium-size cap. "Don't worry about being a good shot; you'll probably never have to draw your weapon. Special cops rarely do."

"Have you ever drawn yours?" I said, trying on the cap.

"Once in five years, as back-up responding to a robbery in progress. Even then, I never had to fire. So relax," he said, smiling and pulling the brim of the cap over my eyes. "We wouldn't think of depriving the students of their favorite English teacher."

I did. All hot summer that holstered gun hung heavy on my hip, but over time it came to matter less. I worked the night shift, assigned to a three-quarters-of-a-mile beat around the boardwalk. Occasionally I broke up crowds after fireworks, directed traffic, and prevented fights outside the local bars and nightclubs. I listened to the boy who lost his bike, and the man searching for his daughter. But mostly I walked, back and forth, up and down the boards. Each night, I signed out six bullets for the police issued .38, and each morning signed them back.

When I started my tour of duty, Jack would make a point of stopping to say hello if he saw me from his patrol car. We'd talk awhile, and he'd usually offer me some coffee from a thermos he kept on the front seat. But as the summer wore on, those visits became less frequent: Jack had other people to visit, other duties to which he had to attend, and I no longer needed his watchful eye. I changed, too. Increasingly, I grew bored with the routine of policing. By August, I no longer worried about whether I would have to use my gun; instead, I found myself listening more and more to the great Atlantic washing the shore. Rather than checking to see if all the store doors were locked, I allowed my mind to drift with the moon over the ocean. Looking at splintered boards under a lamppost, I waited for school to begin.

Weeks passed, and the end of summer approached. The town was particularly festive that year—it was 1976, the bicentennial, and all the hydrants had been painted red, white, and blue. But I had little to do, other than prevent people from walking their dogs on the beach. The hours crawled.

Just before Labor Day, Jack—off duty but still in uniform—stepped into the Quick Check where his fiancée clerked, right into a robbery in progress. Recognized, the two robbers ran; Jack pursued them down the leaf-dark streets and caught up to them by their car. Ordering them to spread their arms out over the hood, he began the routine process of cuffing one robber when, somehow, the other sneaked behind Jack, grabbed his gun, and fired a .38 bullet into his heart. "You bastard, you shot me!" were the last words a neighbor heard him shout.

Jack was twenty-seven. The day after he died, I gave up my police uniform, the gun, the bullets, the boardwalk patrol. The cap I kept. In spring, the small town bloomed: a fountain with the perpetual murmur of running water, lights, holly, an engraved stone to his life. And nothing, even quitting time, was ever routine again.

Theresa Troise Heidel "Evening Iridescence, Shark River"
12" x 16" Watercolor and Gouache 1998 Collection of Judy Page

Theresa Troise Heidel

"Shark River Bridge, Early Evening"
8 1/2" x 11" Watercolor 2000
Collection of Mr. and Mrs. I. and E. Pritchard

"Evening By The Bridge, Shark River"
10" x 15" Watercolor 2000
Collection of Janice Collinson

Theresa Troise Heidel "Belmar Fishing Club"
10" x 24" Watercolor 1989 Collection of Genevieve Di Nardo

Theresa Troise Heidel
"Belmar Fishing Club"
10" x 14" Watercolor 1992

No Snow Day

In memoriam: Joan Brice, friend and teacher 1/20/00.

What tight schedule had you in mind
when the pole rushed to meet you
and short circuited your life? You gave
to everyone—your time, the little money
you had, your love—till it emptied you
and filled them. Each time it emptied you,
your well relined and filled again
until you brimmed with a hug for a downcast
Jack, a crying Jill. Every morning
you made it to school in a van

that broke down in more ways than
it had parts. Yet, you survived it all:
the children sent to schools you could barely afford,
the hours you volunteered to charities,
the priority lists you failed to finish
and the year-end parties you always threw.
You were the empath I saw on "Star Trek" once,
only more talkative. You listened
and absorbed whatever pain a person felt.
They walked away lighter, you heavier

until you dispersed that throb of hurt
to the stars and your God. My son
once predicted snow when it wasn't
forecast. You always remembered and asked
what was he predicting this week. You loved
snow, how it slowed things down, gave you
the time you needed. Tomorrow
a delayed opening; but too late. Who now,
with your permanent absence, will heal this
razor-sharp sorrow that has cut us to the quick?

The First Time

Lisa and her mom wait in the Salvador
Dali-heat for a bus
in Asbury Park. Pigeons bob around
the wire wastebasket. The little girl wades
into a puddle of them and reaches
for the marbly white. Scattering, the pigeons
clap their wings, ascend and flutter into
the cliffy facade of Steinbachs,
their pearly feathers fading into the ledges.
Near the curb, one strut-limps undisturbed by
the bright energy of Lisa's cries. Stay out
of the street, her mom yells. Lisa wants
to know why that pigeon doesn't fly.
Mom thinks it's sick. The three-thirty bus, gray
as the pigeons, glides in late. Lisa screams.
Mom asks what's wrong. *The bus hit the sick one*!
Her mom says it's still there—you just can't see
it. The girl's amazing hazel eyes well up,
No, i saw it, i saw it, i saw it. By the time
they reach Bradley Beach, Lisa has quieted
down, but she cannot connect that smear
of flattened feathers and bone with
the friendly driver. Her mom and all
the other passengers gazing out the windows
as if it were just   another hot day.

Paula Kolojeski "Belmar Boardwalk"
16" x 24" Pastel 1993 Private Collection Prints Available

Autumn Boardwalk In Belmar

There is no story here. If there is, it is the old one that happens every year in late September and early October: the boardwalk stores close, are boarded up. Signs pop up: "Thanks for a great run. See you next summer." The crowds thin, the weather turns colder. Then, after a brief cold spell, Indian summer surprises everyone.

Today is that kind of glorious October day. The trees have spilled a few of their leaves and are beginning to blush in the brilliant sunshine. Political leaflets litter the lawns along with the leaves. Everything seems relaxed and less hectic. What few people remain have come out to walk the boards and lie on the beach. A couple of adventuresome souls swim in the ocean without the protection of lifeguards.

This is a different Belmar from the one I drive through in the summer on the way to the supermarket. In that Belmar, my wife, Barb, has to remind me to keep my eyes on the road. The streets and boardwalk teem with scantily clad young men and women. I try to explain to my wife that it's not really a sexual thing; it's more of a "how-beautiful-they-are" sense of amazement. Somehow I see myself in the crowd at that age. I wonder if these young people even realize how beautiful they are; did I? Recently, I came across a photograph of Barb in her twenties. She had long auburn hair and a slender, curvaceous figure. I said aloud, "Wow, you were beautiful." She replied, "You were at that age, too. You had a washboard stomach, bright eyes, white teeth, and you didn't have to shave but once a week." I guess I look for the ghost of my twenties ambling the boards in the Belmar summer crowd. And in every girl, I catch a part of Barb's youth walking in the sun.

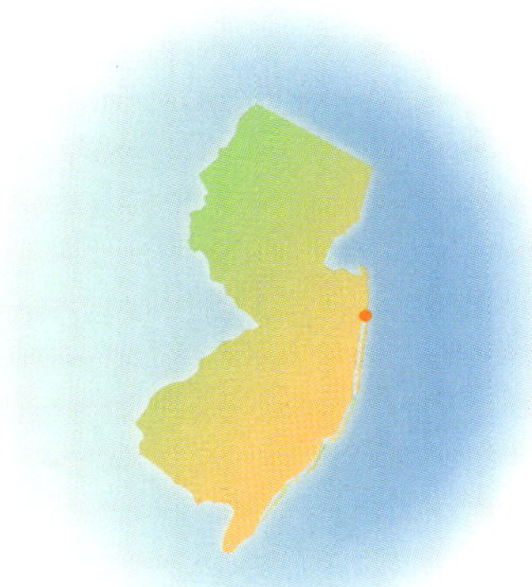

Looking for a place to park along Ocean Avenue is much easier in October, but today, many of the spaces are filled because of the balmy weather. After a brief search, we find one by the boardwalk. We get out and make our way up the ramp, sit on one of the benches facing the ocean. The benches all have small metal plaques dedicated to people. This one reads:

Steve,

Like the ocean your spirit is everlasting.

10/15/82 - 6/18/99

Love, Mom

We wonder who he was and why he left this earth so early in life—one of the boys of summer. Looking at the plate, we realize that October 15 is today. We are somewhat startled by the coincidence. In honor of his birthday, I recite out loud his name and the short yet resonant phrase printed on the plaque. We are overwhelmed by a strong sense that he was loved deeply and that his spirit somehow imbues this enchanting morning by the sea, which now we have come to appreciate even more.

In the small sand dunes between the boardwalk and the beach, seaside goldenrod proliferates with its deep yellow blossoms. Bees bumble in the flowers, and a couple of late-migrating monarch butterflies alight on the flower heads as they make their way south. Across the avenue, orange pumpkin bags hang like ghosts from a wraparound porch. In the front yard, mums in cheering sections of red, yellow, and orange vie for attention.

Two motorcyclists—a male and a female—park their gleaming bikes by the boardwalk, dismount, and take off their helmets. They step up onto the boardwalk. Holding their helmets like the headless horseman holding his head, they ramble over to the railing and stare out at the sea.

A father walks by with his little daughter dressed in sneakers, denim overalls, and a red shirt. She is a lively child with dark hair ringlets. Holding her father's hand, she is singing, "I wanna go down in the sand. I wanna go down in the sand. I wanna go down in the sand." The father says, "No, honey, not today." As they walk on, he relents, taking her down the ramp to the tiny playground on the beach where two swings, a slide, a tunnel, a tire-like swing, and a bridge are enclosed by a snowfence. The girl spins on the tire-like swing while the father watches.

An older mother and father stroll arm-in-arm with their daughter, who looks as if she's in her thirties. The parents are probably from out of town, since the daughter is telling them of places they might like to go for lunch. Later, they stroll back and sit on a bench facing the ocean. The daughter takes off her boots and socks, leaves them with her mom and dad, and goes down to the water to cool off her feet. The parents, dressed in long sleeves, watch her from the bench as they move closer to each other and hold hands.

A man finishes bicycling along the boardwalk, gets off, and goes down to his SUV, where he packs the bike away and takes out a beach chair and towel. Returning to the boardwalk with the towel draped on his shoulders, he carries the beach chair down to the sand, finds "his" spot in the sun, opens the chair, and sits facing the ocean.

There are many bicycles on the boardwalk, from the smallest with training wheels pedaled wildly by a helmeted little boy to a two-wheeler, pedaled by a young mother, with a miniature camper trailer attached. Some bicyclists ride with no hands on the bars, some ride in tandem, and one woman rides with a baby bulldog in her front basket.

There are also many joggers and walkers. One couple, man and woman, jog side by side, their synchronized steps pounding and shaking the boards as they pass. A young father with his shirt off jogs while pushing a tri-wheeled stroller with a child strapped in it. A woman jogs by with a bag of doughnuts in one hand, a half-eaten doughnut in the other. Two older women power-walk, talking about the house near the boardwalk. "If it was like this all the time, we could live here," one says. A man out for the sunshine and fresh salt-air lights up a cigar and walks on. Two in-line skaters glide by him and cough.

The ocean today is agleam with white boats sailing down the last warm days of Indian summer. O Belmar, O beautiful sea that retells itself with each wave, there is no story here, only that of another autumn returning to the Jersey Shore.

Drawbridge

To see a much used road
suddenly raised
is eye-opening. It cries,
"This road that millions
of cars traveled is something
else." Stopped
in our tracks, we are forced
to stare at oil
stains that line it
and the barnacled pilings
that support its hands-in-prayer
opening above
gull blessed boats that slip—laden
with dreams of the big catch—
past our car jammed highways
and out to sea—
Big Marie, Golden Eagle,
Night Hawk...

The Old Mill Inn

In the center of Old Mill Pond, a lone
fisherman stands in a white rowboat,
with a quick flick of his wrist lets his lure
fly. The sun sinks below the leafy tree line,
sets it aflame in the pond. Reflections of ducks
fly over the golden leaf litter and darkening
water. A ripple from some being that
has surfaced to peek at the airy world above
spreads in concentric circles. The trees burn
black now; the fisherman rows back to shore.
The geese and ducks that were paddling around
retreat to their secret harbors. The small
water wheel by the lighted restaurant continues
to turn. Somewhere from the blackened reflection
of trees at the western edge of the pond,
a swan white as a napkin glides out to feed.

Theresa Troise Heidel "St. Catharine's Church, Spring Lake"
7" x 7" Watercolor and Gouache 1995
Collection of the Reverend Monsignor Thomas A. Luebking

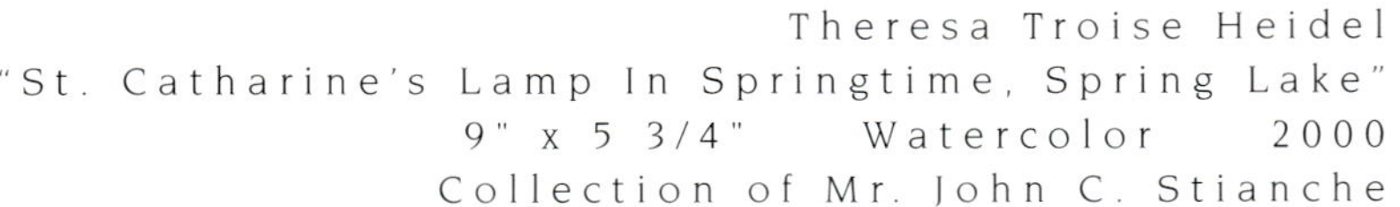

Theresa Troise Heidel
"St. Catharine's Lamp In Springtime, Spring Lake"
9" x 5 3/4" Watercolor 2000
Collection of Mr. John C. Stianche

Theresa Troise Heidel "View Towards The Boardwalk"
12" x 13" Watercolor 1992 Collection of Manny Talaoc

Sue T. Oliver "The Warren Hotel, Spring Lake"
11" x 15" Acrylic 1998 Private Collection Prints Available

Sue T. Oliver "The Beach House, Spring Lake"
11" x 14" Acrylic 1996
Collection of Artist Prints Available

The Grand Hotels

One of my favorite pastimes during the late sixties and early seventies was to walk along Ocean Avenue in Spring Lake. Part of the reason was natural beauty: on one side of the avenue, beyond a spacious boardwalk and beach, the voluminous Atlantic Ocean extended to the horizon, and the steady roll of its whitecapped breakers always soothed my mind. Yet what truly captivated me stood on the opposite side, facing the Atlantic: Spring Lake's grand hotels, whose ornate domes, towers, columns, and gables seemed to rise out of the sand and create an enchanted atmosphere, like that of sandcastles on a beach.

Unfortunately, time has not been kind to three of the most famous: the Monmouth, the Essex and Sussex, and the Warren. Once their elegance and majesty lent an air of grandeur to the whole avenue. Now they are gone, either torn down or abandoned, and their absence can still be felt by those who once knew them.

And still remember...

Taking up a city block, the Monmouth was the largest of the four. One of my sons, when he was in the third grade, would always call it "the mammoth," after the large, extinct elephant that he was then learning about in school. He thought that, because of the animal's size, the hotel must have been named after it. It was an imaginative idea—and wholly plausible.

Like all the grand hotels, the six-story Monmouth was a sight to behold. Built in 1905, the rooftop had dormer windows all around it, as well as a central dome and, toward the front of the building, two polygonal towers. (I was never sure why the towers had been built—lookout points? decoration?—but, as with most architectural flourishes from that era, they gave the hotel a distinctive appearance.) A tall flagpole rose from the middle of the dome, and Old Glory waved in the sea breeze throughout the seasons.

Along the front of the building, the upper floor had a red-brick facade with white-trimmed windows. On the floors below, the bricks changed to a sandy yellow, and a number of the arched windows had white balconies. Over time, the Monmouth came to be one of the most recognized buildings in Spring Lake, partly because of its location. The main entrance of the hotel did not face the ocean; instead, it stood opposite the lake after which the town was named. As such, it became part of a favorite setting for many artists and photographers: Spring Lake in the foreground, a white swan cutting across the surface, and, in the rear, the manicured lawn, circular driveway, and great, columned entrance of the Monmouth—a truly elegant sight. Eight colossal columns, set in pairs, supported an ornate portico. The columns rose about three stories high and had twin spiral designs that crowned their capitals. Those columns seemed as if, like Atlas, they could support the world, and they would never fall.

But fall they did. The Monmouth closed in 1974 because the land was more valuable than the hotel. A year later, the wrecker's ball knocked it down so houses could be built in its place. My wife, Barb, and I stopped there one day after the dust had settled and most of the rubble had been cleared. We looked at each other and sighed. The space the Monmouth had left was almost palpable. While walking by broken bricks and splintered sticks, a glint from the rubble caught Barb's eye. She bent down and picked up a key attached to a piece of oblong cowhide, imprinted on which was *Room 316 Monmouth*. We still have it—a key to a vanished era.

Looking at that key now and feeling between my fingers the stiff, smooth cowhide and the cold metal, it opens the creaky door of my memory. I think of driving or walking past the Monmouth, and how Barb would tell our sons about the formal ballroom dances, the live orchestras, and the famous people who attended dinners there. Always the boys would be impressed and want to go to such events. "Perhaps when you're older," their mother would say. Then their attention would turn back to the small Matchbox cars they had brought with them.

On the next block, north of the Monmouth, stood the six-story Essex and Sussex. Together, the two hotels dominated Ocean Avenue: they were like two anchored ocean liners, commanding the attention of anyone who walked by. Tourists would stop to look. Some took pictures.

The Essex and Sussex presented a vision of symmetry. Two gable-roofed, red-brick extensions anchored the ends, each with a three-story, white-columned porch, each mirroring the other. Between the two extensions and the front entrance ran two long, recessed portions of the hotel, each with five identical rows of windows, each with white trim stunningly set against the light yellow brick. But it was the front entrance—the grand front entrance—that dominated the Essex and Sussex. Stone steps led to six paired, white Ionic columns, each of which rose three stories to a railed porch. Three more stories of red brick façade and white-trimmed windows were topped by a mansard roof with triple dormer windows built into each side and topped by a gold-tinctured cupola.

The hotel even served as a backdrop in a couple of movies: *Ragtime* (1981) and *Once Upon A Time In America* (1984). Barb and I were delighted to discover in those films the hotel that we passed so often—even though we never went in. We never needed to reserve a room at the Essex and Sussex, since we lived only a few towns away, in Bradley Beach. The opportunity to attend a party there never arose, either. And as for dining, there were cheaper places to go on our meager budget. We

Sue T. Oliver "Essex And Sussex"
12" x 18" Acrylic 2000 Private Collection

were admirers from afar.

Still, it was like seeing an old friend every time we passed. And perhaps, as in some friendships, we took it for granted. We assumed it would always be there. But in 1984, the eighty-five-year-old hotel closed. Condominiums were all the rage, and the new owners wanted to capitalize on the trend. However, their planned, two-hundred-six-room hotel-condominium never opened, and in 1993 other owners took over, intending to turn the building into luxury senior-citizen apartments.

As I write this, in fall 2000, the place still remains closed, and it appears more run down, paler, than ever before. Its picture-postcard days when wealthy shore people attended the formal balls, reserved rooms, and took in the ocean's bracing salt-tonic and the lake's tranquility seem to be over. On the north side of the Essex and Sussex, a pattern of vines straggle up the wall, and a high cyclone fence guards the perimeter of the building.

Gargoyles. I first spotted them perched on the roof of the Warren Hotel's Beach House in the 1970s, and each time I passed thereafter I was beguiled into seeing if they were still there. It excited my imagination to know that this house from another era had mythical creatures inhabiting its rooftop.

The Victorian-style Beach House was about four stories high with brown cedar shakes and white trim. A porch with small white columns curved languidly around its first floor, and its roof had many of the prerequisite Victorian accoutrements, in addition to gargoyles: gables, turrets, and two brick chimneys. I later discovered that the ridges in the roof were occupied by terra-cotta griffins, and that the house was once owned by a poet in the 1890s. Ah, those poets. No wonder I felt drawn to the house.

This past summer, to my dismay, I learned that the Warren Hotel and its Beach House were going to go the way of the Monmouth, with the land being divided into eleven tracts for housing. Barb and I decided in December that, before those Victorian structures could be sucked into the black hole of the past, we would pay a visit. Located a few blocks north of the Essex and Sussex, the Warren's Tudor-style wood-frame structure, with its bell-shaped central roof and conical towers on either end, immediately brought us back in time. We walked up the wooden front steps to a porch with maroon indoor/outdoor carpeting and a row of white wicker chairs, perfect for spending long, idle hours by the sea.

As we entered the front door, the gentleman at the desk asked if we had reservations. We told him we just wanted to look through the hotel—to pay our last respects, as it were. He said they were having their last wedding that afternoon—"two hundred guests, a small wedding." However, since guests had not begun arriving yet, he would allow us to walk around. Pointing to the banquet room across from the desk, he suggested we start there.

Upon opening the door to the dining area, we felt a sharp drop in temperature. I thought of the thousands of weddings that must have taken place here over the years. We looked at the twenty round, wooden tables with cane chairs all empty now, and Barb shuddered with a chill. The hairs on the back of her neck stood on end. She whispered, "I can almost feel the lives of the people that have passed through here."

"Yeah," I replied. "It reminds me of the hotel in *The Shining*."

We moved to the lobby, which was full of wicker and antiques. A Victorian Christmas tree, complete with a gold bow on the top branch and decorated with pearls, angels, and camellias, lent a warmer, friendlier spirit to the place. Barb seated herself in a hooded, cobra-like wicker chair that she fell

Sue T. Oliver "Monmouth Hotel, Lakeside"
10" x 15" Acrylic 2000 Private Collection

Sue T. Oliver "Monmouth Hotel, Oceanside"
10" x 15" Acrylic 2000
Private Collection Prints Available

in love with instantly. "I want to buy this when they auction off the furniture," she said. I sighed; it was difficult to visualize this place being dismantled piece by piece, then sold off to the highest bidder. I tried not to think about the final torment: the wrecker's ball.

Leaving the lobby, we ambled down Peacock Alley, a carpeted, wide, furnished hallway that led to the other side of the hotel. Along the hallway, crystal chandeliers hung from the ceiling, and the walls were decorated with framed paintings. At one point we passed a locked E. Patricia Molloy Room. I wondered what would happen to her bronze dedication plaque, which commemorated the one who "left her indelible mark in the history of the Warren Hotel."

Before leaving, we stopped at the Beach House to look up at its gargoyles and griffins. A man and woman were photographing the house from different perspectives. I fantasized that they might be from some big, glossy magazine, perhaps doing a photo essay. In reality, they were probably like Barb and me, getting one last look at a unique house that would soon fade into history.

Driving out of town, I wondered who might buy the gargoyles and griffins. Even if someone did, it would be similar to taking an animal from its natural habitat and placing it in a showcase: the effect just wouldn't be the same. Good-bye, my gargoyles. Good-bye, my grand hotels. Good-bye. Good-bye.

Dick LaBonté "Spring Lake 1892"
20" x 24" Acrylic 1992
Collection of Spring Lake Community Theater
Prints Available

Susan Walsh McLean "Generations"
10 1/2" x 14" Watercolor 1999 Collection of Linda and Richard Yeni Prints Available

Susan Walsh McLean "Old Timers"
11" x 14" Watercolor 2000

Private Collection Prints Available

Pauline Mickle "Commercial Fishing Boats, Point Pleasant Beach"
13" x 22" Watercolor 2000 Collection of Artist Prints Available

Pauline Mickle

"Ellie B"
14 1/2" x 10" Watercolor and Marker 1997
Private Collection Prints Available

"Sea Wanderer"
14" x 20" Watercolor 1999
Collection of Artist Prints Available

CHAPTER 2

Dennis Foy "Manasquan River Sunset"
30" x 24" Oil 2000 Private Collection Prints Available

Paula Kolojeski "Main Beach, Manasquan"
16" x 24" Pastel 1995 Private Collection Prints Available

Paula Kolojeski

"Sea Watch Beach, Manasquan"
16" x 24" Pastel 1996
Private Collection
Prints Available

"Riddle Way, Manasquan"
16" x 24" Pastel 1995
Private Collection
Prints Available

Susan Walsh McLean "Morning At Manasquan Beach"
10 1/4" x 14 1/8" Watercolor 2000 Private Collection Prints Available

Susan Walsh McLean "Gee – Gee's"
11" x 14" Watercolor 2000
Private Collection Prints Available

Paula Kolojeski "Lucky's, Point Pleasant"
16" x 24" Pastel 1993 Private Collection Prints Available

It Was A Very Good House

The place was so different, I almost missed it. The two-story Colonial, once shadowed by mimosas and fronted by lilacs, had been replaced by a squat savings bank. Where children had run about in a wide open yard, now cars pulled in and out of a parking lot. Only a few cottonwoods and lilacs had survived.

I was amazed. I hadn't traveled busy Bridge Avenue in several years, but when I did I would always pass that yellow Colonial and give it a long, wistful glance, remembering my many visits there, all of them idyllic. Though the surrounding area had changed over time, I thought the house would always remain. But now, inching with a long line of other cars toward Bay Head, I approached Dorsett Dock Road—and couldn't believe it. The house where my brother and his wife had lived for nearly two decades, where I had played with my five nieces and spent so many holidays, where I had enjoyed some of the best moments of my young life—it was gone, all gone. More surprising was the pang of loss I felt. Even though I hadn't seen the house in several years and those good times were well in the past, the house's disappearance seemed to open up a hole inside me—as if a rock had been dislodged, exposing long-forgotten memories. I hadn't planned to stop, but suddenly I found myself pulling onto Dorsett Dock Road and into the parking lot.

It was an ordinary Saturday morning, and the lot held nothing to draw in anyone other than the bank's normal customers. Cars idled at the drive-up window, people parked and hurriedly walked to the front door, summertime traffic trickled past. I parked behind the bank and, amid some odd stares, ambled to the middle of the lot. Looking around, I spotted the cottonwood tree, taller now, that I used to see from what was once my older brother and his wife's bedroom window. I was twenty-one then; they were in their mid-thirties, with four girls and one more on the way, the oldest fourteen. The time was the mid-1960s, when Point Pleasant borough offered a quiet, semi-rural life. It had a small school, large and green yards, and a few businesses that provided the necessary basics—food, clothing, gas, and little else. As many people do, my brother and his wife had built their lives here on the shambles of their past: his throw-away first marriage and political career as head of the Young Republicans Club; her failed marriage to escape the orphanage in her native Jamaica; their complete break from their families shortly after marrying; and their move to Puerto Rico to escape the resulting anger.

In Point Pleasant they put all that behind them. Within a few years after moving, they had reached their optimum point of happiness: the girls obedient and in school; he a respected insurance agent in Manhattan; she a local mover and shaker who knew all the right people. He had a keen mind for figures and an ability to listen, to make others feel they could trust him. She had a knack for eliciting little-known details from the lives of influential people—a judge, the school superintendent, the police chief—while still maintaining an aura of mystery around herself. Together, they seemed to have it all. When he came home weary after his two-hour commute from Manhattan, she would meet him at the last train stop, drive him home, and have a huge chuck steak and fries ready for him. The two oldest girls would wash and dry the dishes.

I lived with them one summer in 1965, until I found a winter rental five minutes from their home. Thanksgiving, Christmas, Easter...I spent the holidays with them that first year in Jersey. At Christmas, they made me a part of their local caroling group, and on Christmas Eve I took charge of putting lights around the outside trees. I even provided my own contribution to the festivities: a Lionel train set that I had had since a boy. I took great joy in seeing my nieces put together the tracks, and in seeing the shining black cars revolve under new sets of eyes. My brother, my sister-in-law, their daughters—they were my family, their house a light against the dark.

And how they loved that house. Having found a true home, they lavished it with attention, adding a patio, a pool, and a cabana. They landscaped it with lilac bushes, mimosa trees, a cascade of wisteria draped over a wooden fence bordering their yard. My brother oversaw the larger construction projects, while she planted, fed, watered, and cared for the shrubs and flowers. I would often see her kneeling by a lilac bush, her watering can in hand. As she sprinkled the leaves, she softly spoke to them. The star-like clusters of purple trembled under the drops, and the incense of their fragrance haloed the air around the bush. In the church of her garden, she went from bush to bush as though she were a priestess of the lilacs, blessing each one.

That summer I stayed with them, we would sprawl out in lawn chairs on clear nights and gaze at the country stars.

"You know what I'd really like to do," I said one night. "Go to Alaska to lay pipe and write."

Stroking Duke, the German Shepherd that lay by his side, my brother sighed. "You're such a dreamer," he said. "Me, I'd like to have my own business in this area, so I wouldn't have to commute four hours a day to New York and back. Think of all the time and money I'd save."

Another night, my brother said, "Did you know Eugene O'Neill, the famous playwright, lived here at one time?"

"No," I said. "Where?"

"A little west of here. I heard he even wrote a play here, but they never found it. Ya see?" he said, poking my arm. "You don't have to go to Alaska to write. Besides, it's too cold there."

We'd talk like this, the insects and frogs loud around us, until the night coolness and dampness nudged us back into

Linda Hejduk "Lovelandtown Bridge And River Belle"
11" x 14" Watercolor 2000 Collection of Artist Prints Available

the lighted house.

Sometimes, on sun-high days, I'd mow their lawn. My two oldest nieces would follow me around, and as they did I'd tell them stories about the Mad Mower.

"Why did they call him the Mad Mower?" Ginny, the younger of the two, asked one time.

"Because he had a long beard and was always mowing lawns for money. He had no family, and this was the only job he had," I said.

"How did he survive in the winter?" Lily, my fourteen-year-old niece, wanted to know.

"He shoveled snow."

"Did they ever call him the Mad Shoveler?" Ginny asked.

"No. It was always the Mad Mower," I said. "People thought him weird because he'd talk to the grass. But they could never quite hear what he said above the noise of the lawnmower. Some said he was predicting the future, and telling the grass what would happen in years to come. They said that, over time, the grass gave up its secrets to the wind—and that, even today, the wind still carries the Mad Mower's whispered predictions; all you have to do is listen hard."

When I cut the last swath of grass, we ran into the house, donned our bathing suits, and walked barefoot down the dusty road to the river beach. All the way, the girls would listen to the wind, and try to hear the whispered secrets of tomorrow.

They always failed, of course, or at least I hope they did. Change, like the sun, touches everything, and so it did with my brother and his family—unkindly. Eventually, he started his own business and stopped commuting to New York. He made more money, and she began taking trips to her native Jamaica. They bought a three-story mansion in West Long Branch. She hired a maid to clean it. He got involved with another woman at work. She got involved helping a poor family in Jamaica and went there more frequently. The younger girls went to private school and took for granted what they had: the designer clothes, a huge swimming pool with accessories, the fine restaurants they ate in, the mansion they lived in.

I began to see all of them less and less. During one visit, I discovered on the mantlepiece the locomotive from my train set.

"How did this get here?" I asked my sister-in-law, who was busy sorting through tile samples for the kitchen.

"Oh, I don't know," she said distractedly. "I think it belonged to a train set the kids used to have. All the other pieces are either lost or broken."

Later, I asked about her gardening. She said they had a gardener who came in once a week. "The place is just too big for me," she explained.

After a while, I stopped seeing them completely; I had married and moved farther away, and it seemed none of us ever had time to get together. A few years later, I found out my brother was up on charges of fraud involving his business. By then, they had both separated and were into other marriages. Their children, for the most part, were into divorces of their own. The days of Point Pleasant had long gone by.

But, standing there in the parking lot, I suddenly found myself retracing history. I went from room to room in their non-existent house, walked casually around their now-asphalted yard. I imagined sitting under the clear stars, talking with my brother about Alaska and writing and Eugene O'Neill. I was a rock in a river that rushed over me. Then, while walking along the perimeter of the parking lot, I spotted a lilac bush. Kneeling down as if in prayer, I touched the star-like clusters, their fragrance blessing the air. For a long time, I did not move.

Paula Kolojeski "Point Pleasant South"
12" x 18" Pastel 1998 Private Collection Prints Available

Paula Kolojeski "Badge Booth, Point Pleasant"
16" x 24" Pastel 2000
Private Collection Prints Available

Dede Esenlohr "Clustered Together – Twilight Lake"
13" x 22" Acrylic 1992 Collection of C. Bekes, M.D.

Dede Esenlohr "The Footbridge"
18" x 26" Acrylic 1990
Collection of H. Westin Clarke, Jr.

The Monarchs

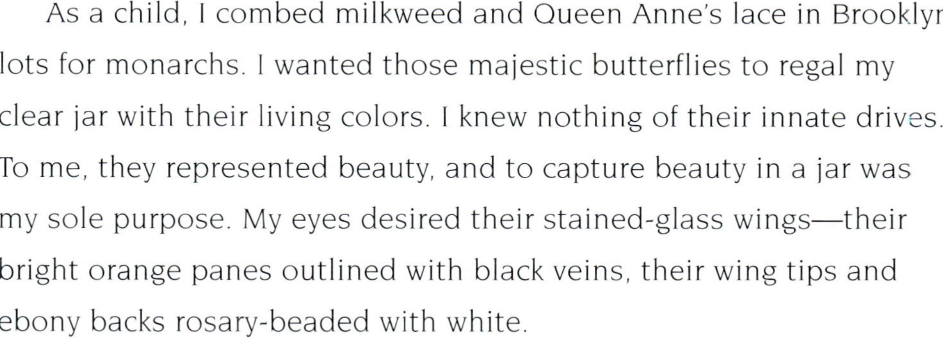

As a child, I combed milkweed and Queen Anne's lace in Brooklyn lots for monarchs. I wanted those majestic butterflies to regal my clear jar with their living colors. I knew nothing of their innate drives. To me, they represented beauty, and to capture beauty in a jar was my sole purpose. My eyes desired their stained-glass wings—their bright orange panes outlined with black veins, their wing tips and ebony backs rosary-beaded with white.

Stalking one creature, I waited until it landed on a flower head. I sneaked behind it, watched its wings pulse open, close, open, close—then picked it from the flower, its closed wings between my index finger and thumb. I placed it in my jar with a few blades of grass and the flower head it had been sipping on. After plucking several monarchs, my thumb and index prints turned iridescent from the powder of their wings.

Later I showed my colorful catch to my mother, who turned from the kitchen sink, wiped her hands, and held the jar up to the light. She said they were beautiful, but I should really let them go. They needed to be free.

I now live at the Jersey Shore, and I still love to watch the monarchs. Every year I observe them flitting from goldenrod to goldenrod on the dunes of Seaside and Island Beach, drifting southward in the warm air mass. I remember one day in late summer when, while driving down Route 35 in Bay Head, I spotted a number of monarchs fluttering over the highway like scraps of blown paper and settling on the bushes and butterfly plants of the nearby gardens. Another time, in early fall in Cape May, I was astonished by a tree filled with monarchs that seemed to be resting before they moved on. They became one with the tree, pulsing their wings now here, now there. Many more monarchs were flitting haphazardly from bush to plant, feeling their way toward the Delaware Bay, searching for the best place in which to cross.

Over the years, I have discovered that monarchs migrate annually from Canada to Mexico. A migrating insect, especially one as fragile as the monarch, seems absurd. Terns migrate, caribou migrate, but butterflies? Not only do they migrate, but they fly all the way down to Mexico, where they winter in the fir forests of the volcanic highlands (ten thousand feet above sea level), about a four-hour drive west of Mexico City. Sometimes the branches are so loaded with the broods, they break and fall.

Every year I am reminded of how far the monarchs must go with their paper-thin wings, which measure barely four inches, and of the many dangers (storms, predators, frost, traffic) they must face. Many will perish, but millions more will make it to the highlands of Mexico, where they will blossom in trees far from our winter. Around early March depending on the weather, they will begin their northward migration. Along the way they will stop to breed, and their progeny will continue northward, perhaps stopping to breed themselves. It is the rare monarch that makes it all the way back to where it started, but there have been a few, as evidenced by the tags scientists have placed on their wings.

Once, in mid-October, I tramped the beach in Lavallette looking for unusual shells along the tideline. With the waves crashing in on one side and a wide expanse of sand on the other, I thought I was alone until I glanced up and spotted a single monarch fluttering south. I thought of how I would be wary of taking my late-model car all the way to Mexico, yet this late-migrating monarch—which weighs half as much as a small paper clip—is urged to make an over-a-thousand-miles journey with nothing more than its innate drive and its wisp of a body. And to think I once confined these creatures to a jar. I wished this one God-speed, for this world could always use a little more beauty, no matter how small.

Metamorphosis

She hid
caterpillars
in rusted cans,
put the open end
in a hole
of the wall.
No escape. Yet
they drew breath...
What did she know
of mysteries? Days
later, kneeling before
the wall, she found
no caterpillars
in the untouched can.
Now she searches
the world for butterflies.

Dick LaBonté "Sunday Afternoon Bathers"
24" x 32" Acrylic 1978 Collection of Artist Prints Available

Virginia Perle "Boardwalk, Seaside Park"
10" x 16" Watercolor 1999 Private Collection

Virginia Perle "Sunset, Seaside Park"
7" x 11" Watercolor 1999
Private Collection

Seaside

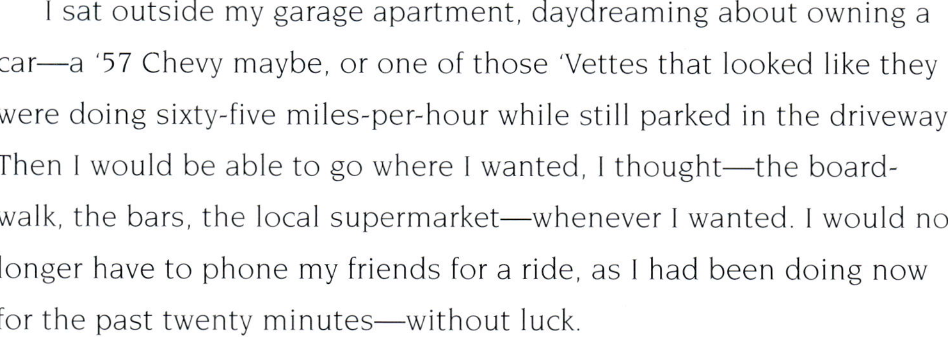

I sat outside my garage apartment, daydreaming about owning a car—a '57 Chevy maybe, or one of those 'Vettes that looked like they were doing sixty-five miles-per-hour while still parked in the driveway. Then I would be able to go where I wanted, I thought—the boardwalk, the bars, the local supermarket—whenever I wanted. I would no longer have to phone my friends for a ride, as I had been doing now for the past twenty minutes—without luck.

It was Memorial Day, 1965. Fresh out of college, I had moved to Point Pleasant from New York a few months earlier; I had had no desire to return to my mother's small apartment in Brooklyn, plus I had heard the pace of living was slower along the shore. But I hadn't counted on it moving at an inchworm's crawl. Arriving in the off-season, I found the fronts of stores, restaurants, and bars layered with bulky boards. Traffic lights blinked at near-empty intersections. I could walk entire blocks without seeing another human being.

But after months of living the cloistered life, circumstances began to change. The local businesses opened their cobwebbed windows to sunlight. Trees along Arnold Avenue blossomed. Traffic lights stopped blinking and turned green, amber, and red. At the pubs, loud people packed in four and five deep at the bar, shouting above louder music. The seasonal migration had begun, with its waves near tidal proportions. Opportunities abounded.

For those with cars, that is. On one of the busiest weekends of the year, I sat in an old lawnchair on a baking, cracked-tar driveway, counting the cars that zoomed along the street and wishing I owned every one of them. I watched them pass: a '58 Ford Fairlaine...a '61 Chevy Impala...a '59 Ford convertible—and I was up, racing down the driveway, shouting at the top of my lungs: "GIIINAAA!!"

The convertible's tailights flared and the car skidded to a quick stop. The driver, a pretty young woman with long brown hair, turned around, saw me waving frantically on the sidewalk, and smiled.

"Frank!" she yelled. She put the car in reverse and pulled up to the curb, stopping in front of me. I couldn't believe it: my cousin Gina had arrived from the Bronx on one of those migratory waves, like a gift from the gods. Six years older than I, Gina was the one who babysat me when I was a boy, and she was always my favorite cousin. She listened to my stories about school or trying out for sports teams or the fights I had had with friends, and she always seemed to care about what I said. Now here she was, in the flesh.

"I didn't know you lived so close by," she said, her brown eyes flashing. "We're renting a bungalow for the week only a few blocks over. What are the odds!" She introduced me to her friends, Maria and Maggie, each of whom automatically brushed back her hair and smiled in greeting. Maria looked a little like Elizabeth Taylor, with her violet eyes, black hair, and svelte yet busty figure. Maggie, the shortest of the three, had freckles and red hair. I waved at them both.

"So what are you up to?" Gina asked, poking my belly. "What big plans does the bachelor have tonight?"

Before I could answer, Maggie piped up, "Why don't you come with us to Seaside Heights? Do you like to dance?"

"He must if he's related to Gina," Maria giggled.

Gina looked at her quickly, then back at me. She smiled. "How 'bout it, knighthood? Think you can keep up with some older women?"

I paused. "Sure, why not. It might be fun. Just give me a minute." I strolled up the driveway, hands in my pockets, trying to keep a steady pace. As soon as I entered my apartment, I dashed into my bedroom, slapped on some Old Spice, changed my shirt, and brushed back my hair; I refrained from yelling out a "WHOOPEE!" Within minutes I was back outside, trying not to look too excited.

"Jump in," Gina said, clearing a couple of damp towels from the back seat, next to Maggie. I did, and we were off.

At the bungalow where they were staying, the girls spent a few hours showering, changing clothes, and preening before the one full-length mirror in the house. By the time we were ready to leave, it was nightfall.

"First we're going to the Hoffman House," Gina said. "Start things off right." Located on the boardwalk in Point Pleasant Beach, the Hoffman House was a nightclub popular for its dancing, drinking, and flirting; I had never been there before, but apparently Gina, Maria, and Maggie had—many times. When we arrived, they seemed to recognize everyone in the club. They were all part of the "Bunglow Bunch," and they all knew the same people—"Didn't we meet at Don's party?" "Jack? He's all right. He came with that group from Bay Ridge." At the very least, they knew where a person was staying. Dressed to the nines, the three girls were in demand on the dance floor as soon as we entered. They danced the Swim, the Twist, and the Mashed Potato. Gina, with her brown hair, brown eyes, and powerful yet curvy build, was the most spirited of the three and the best dancer.

I sat at the table, drinking a Manhattan and watching the three of them on the dance floor. It felt good to be in the company of these three older women, even though Gina had introduced me to everyone as "her little cousin Frank from Point Pleasant." During a dance break, Gina and her girlfriends returned to the bar a little breathless. She asked me what I was drinking.

"You're sure he's old enough to drink?" Maggie asked.

Although I was twenty-one, I looked about sixteen and felt self-conscious about my boyish looks, especially in a crowd of older people.

Dick LaBonté "The Twenties"
24" x 30" Acrylic 1992 Collection of Mr. and Mrs. Edward J. Smith Prints Available

Gina replied, "Yeah. He's a big boy now."

After this brief but humiliating conversation, I ordered a martini. Gina said she would pay for the round.

"I thought you were drinking Manhattans?" she asked.

"I was, but now I want to try a martini," I said. I was enjoying my freedom.

"You shouldn't mix your drinks like that. You'll make yourself sick."

"Don't worry about me," I boasted, my voice full of self-assurance. "I have a cast-iron stomach. Besides, I'm a big boy now."

"Okay," Gina sighed. "I just don't want to see you get sick."

After another set, the girls wanted to move on to a nightclub closer to Seaside Heights, so we all left. With Gina driving, we went cruising down the barrier island on Route 35 South. To our right, the moon shone on Barnegat Bay. White sails of boats triangled the dark. The salty, warm air carried a whiff of honeysuckle in it, as the breeze in the convertible whipped my hair. I leaned back in the seat and smiled; after two drinks, I was feeling warm and fuzzy. And why not? I was with three attractive older women, I was twenty-one, and the world stretched out before me filled with possibilities. And Gina would always be there to look out for me, I was sure of it.

After a few miles, we hit Seaside Heights. Cramped streets were filled with car upon car, crushing in on each other, all cruising for a parking space and a chance to be seen in the hot neon air. We looked at the throngs of people spilling off the sidewalks, all of whom looked back at us with equal fascination. Seaside Heights, the Rio de Janeiro of the Jersey Shore. With summer clothes as their costumes, crowds of young people paraded up and down the main streets and boardwalk. Rock music blared out of every nightclub where Shore bands played: "*I can't get no satisfaction, though I tried, and I tried, and I tried, and I tried*...I CAN'T GET NO..." And the crowds played the part, looking and searching for someone or something they couldn't name.

After finally finding a spot in one of the meter-forested parking lots, we trooped up to the boardwalk. "I'm hungry," Gina said as soon as we stepped onto the weathered boards. She pointed to one of the piers that stretched out over the ocean. "There's a food stand over there." I knew better than to argue with Gina when she wanted food; besides, I was feeling a bit hungry myself. I followed, though a bit unsteadily, tripping over a couple of raised boards. The drinks had apparently been more potent than I first thought. Maggie and Maria looked at each other and grinned.

A kaleidoscope of lights surrounded us as we walked onto the pier: the stilted lights of the roller coaster, the pendulum lights of the gondola ride, the myriad and multicolored neon lights of the stands, and the grand circle of light itself, the Ferris wheel—a radial of stars. A shower of sparks rained from the wiregrill ceiling of the bumper car rides. The pungent odor of electricity filled the air, as did the shrill screams from the people in the bumper cars. At the entrance to the Fun House, the fat lady laughed on cue.

At the food stand, Gina and I both ordered sausage-and-pepper sandwiches and beer. I watched the swells of children, running around the legs of their parents, and I began to feel a little maudlin. "Gina," I asked, "do you remember one winter when there was a lot of snow on the ground, and you put me on your Flexible Flyer and pulled me around the streets? I laid back and looked up at my white breath and the puffy clouds."

"No," she said as the counterman gave us our orders.

"Oh." I took a sip of my beer, spilling a little on my shirt.

As Gina took out her compact mirror to check her makeup, Maggie asked in a hushed voice, "Is your cousin going to be

Linda Hejduk "Morning News"
11" x 14" Watercolor 1998 Collection of Artist Prints Available

all right?" Gina just rolled her eyes.

Not far from us, the rattle and clatter of the roller coaster sounded as it climbed the first, high hill; then the screech of voices as the cars thundered down and screamed around the first hairpin turn. I could feel the rumble vibrate up from the planks of the pier into the soles of my shoes, up my leg bones and hips and into the pit of my stomach, while I shivered in the heat. Through the din, I caught the calliope of the carousel, as a menagerie of wooden horses, tigers, lions, and giraffes whirled in their circular chase and created a persistent breeze in the humid air.

"Gina," I said, trying to talk around a large slice of sausage I had just bitten off, "did you ever think when you babysat me twelve years ago that we'd be here now, drinking beer together and eating sandwiches?"

Gina looked at me out of the corner of her eye. "No, Frank. Don't talk with your mouth full."

I chewed thoughtfully. Life certainly held its surprises.

Finishing our sandwiches and beer, we walked down to the nearest nightclub, and into a brightly colored mass of humanity. I sat at the bar and ordered a gin and tonic—something lighter for a change of pace—while Gina, Maggie, and Maria went immediately to the dance floor. They shimmied and shook with a succession of partners, as the bar vibrated with bass, drums, and guitar. When the set ended, someone shouted, "Last call!" and the girls returned to the bar, perspiring. They exchanged numbers with the last guys they had danced with, and I ordered one final drink, a sloe gin fizz.

"Hey, Frank," Gina said, "you sure about that?"

"Sure," I answered. "After all, I'm a big boy." Gina shook her head.

The manager turned up the lights in the club, and the remaining patrons moaned. "Closing in ten minutes. Finish up, please," he yelled. After about a minute of discussing where to go, the three girls decided on the O. B. Diner back in Point Pleasant Beach. Just about all the summer bungalow people knew of the O. B.: it was the place to go to eat and socialize after the nightclubs closed. The food was decent, the prices fair, and the service quick. I quickly gulped down my drink, and we joined the procession edging toward the doors.

Outside, the crowds had thinned. There was a slight chill in the air. We all walked over to the railing of the boardwalk for fresh air. Our clothes reeked of smoke. Before us, the Atlantic washed in the moonlight and starlight as it had done eons ago. Under the halo of the boardwalk lights, I looked out as far as my eyes would allow, trying to peer into the years waiting ahead. I wished that the moon were a crystal ball.

"Gina, where do you think we'll be twelve years from now?" I said. The stars seemed to be whirling above me.

Gina looked at her two friends and smiled. "I don't know, Frank."

"I'll have a car by then."

"Uh-uh.

"And you'll be married, maybe." The stars were whirling faster, as were the boardwalk lights.

She sighed. "Maybe. I don't know. Why all the questions, knighthood?" She turned to me. "Frank?"

I heard her, but I didn't answer. My head felt like the Seaside carousel, and my stomach had leapt into my throat. Someone took me by the arm and led me down the steps to the beach, then I was on my knees among the creosote pilings of the boardwalk, wretching violently. With each heave, I could hear the surf boom along the shoreline—a hard, unforgiving sound.

When it was over, I looked up. Gina was standing over me, barefoot, her shoes dangling in one hand.

"How's that cast-iron stomach now?"

I grimaced. "Guess I'm not such a big boy."

Gina smiled weakly. "I tried to tell you."

I crawled out from underneath the boards and stood up. Overhead, some light clouds obscured part of the moon's face. I no longer felt warm and fuzzy inside, just embarrassed. Gina came up next to me.

"Hey, knighthood, I have a confession to make," she said. Her voice was a pale whisper that I could barely hear over the surf. "Remember when you asked me about carrying you on my Flexible Flyer?"

"Yeah?"

"Well, I do remember. I remember thinking you were the cutest little kid, so sweet and sensitive. And I remember thinking that you were the best cousin I could ever hope for."

I looked at her. "And now?"

"And now I think you're a wonderful young man, who has many adventures and wonderful times waiting for him. And you're still the best cousin I could ever hope for."

The clouds passed, and I saw the moon clearly in each of her eyes. Looking into them, I imagined all the futures possible, all those adventures and wonderful times waiting for me. Whichever became real, I knew that this moment—my cousin Gina standing before me, young and vibrant, her brown hair blowing carelessly around her face as the ocean swept up along the sand—would always remain with me.

"Thanks for taking me along tonight, Gina," I said.

She smiled and offered her hand. "Let's go," she said. Hand in hand, cousins, we walked back up to the boardwalk and, with her friends following, back down the ramp and into the dark, narrow sidestreets of Seaside. I wouldn't be going to the O. B. tonight, but that was all right. I had time.

Dick LaBonté "Girls' Sneakbox Race"
24" x 30" Acrylic 1982
Collection of Mr. and Mrs. Gary F. Thorpe
Prints Available

Ludlow Thorston "Beaton's – Winter"
13 1/2" x 20" Watercolor 2000 Collection of Mr. and Mrs. Charles Vigorita

Ludlow Thorston "Beaton's Boatyard"
14" x 21" Watercolor 2000
Collection of Mr. and Mrs. Charles Vigorita

A Winter's Sketch

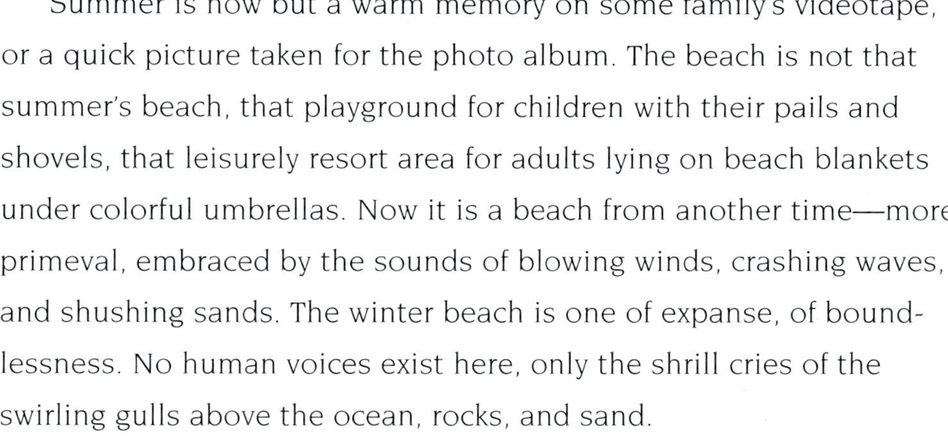

Summer is now but a warm memory on some family's videotape, or a quick picture taken for the photo album. The beach is not that summer's beach, that playground for children with their pails and shovels, that leisurely resort area for adults lying on beach blankets under colorful umbrellas. Now it is a beach from another time—more primeval, embraced by the sounds of blowing winds, crashing waves, and shushing sands. The winter beach is one of expanse, of boundlessness. No human voices exist here, only the shrill cries of the swirling gulls above the ocean, rocks, and sand.

There is an elemental, unraked beauty to the desolate winter beach. The sand ripples over the once-clear boardwalk that leads onto it. The tiny grains pile up along the ribbed snowfences, leaving only the stark tops of their posts showing. Farther out, along the beach, the sand rises and dips and swirls into patterns that only an artist could create, a perfect wildness. The wind howls, and the sand responds. Everything is in flux. The beach you step on today will not be the same one you step on tomorrow. But you will never know it. Nature repeats itself endlessly, ever changing, ever unchanged.

Along the tideline, the rough waters bite into the shoreline, leaving foot-high, cliff-like escarpments. Just before it, thousands of shards of shells have been blown upright like tiny tombstones, each with its own miniature dune formed behind it. In fact, the calligraphy of the entire strand is cluttered with scallop and clam shells, dark-blue mussels, crab bits, shiny egg cases of black skate, tangles of brown seaweed. There is also the glitter of beach glass: turquoise, amber, bright emerald...beautiful gems born of sand and polished by the sea. The waves rush in, and a piece of driftwood humps up out of the sand like an out-of-place python, inspecting its surroundings.

A lone figure—a woman in a dark, hooded coat—braves the weather and needle-sharp wind. Near an ice-bearded jetty, she stops and stoops to pick up some object from the tide. Rising and straightening herself, she looks into her gloved hand at a smooth piece of frosted-blue sea glass—a rarity. A sharp wind whitecaps the waves. Farther out, a flock of geese fly south parallel to the shore. They are like cloves against the pewter-colored ocean and the wispy-white, arctic sea smoke that erases the horizon. The immensity of ocean and sky envelop the geese; one can almost sense their small, warm heartbeats as they fly toward their destination. It evokes lines from a poem by William Cullen Bryant: *"All day thy wings have fanned / At that far height, the cold, thin atmosphere..."*

Shadows inch from the shells, pool in the shallows of the sand, slowly overtake the beach. The woman watches. She holds the blue glass firmly in her hand. Overhead, the first stars appear, faint yet clear. Shadows deepen toward night, and the wind cuts across the beach like a scythe. The woman doesn't move. She closes her eyes. Through a frozen sea of thoughts, memory breaks free—days of crowded beaches, of bathers rushing through the endless breakers, of a man, alone in the surf, who offers his hand. The tide flows around his feet, his skin is slightly tanned, and his smile shines as brightly as the miniature suns glittering along the waves. Slowly, her memories emerge, and with them a yearning for the summer that was, the summer that is yet to come.

A Winter's Night

From the steam-heated womb of our living room, we push out—
dwarf explorers of Snow White. Boreas plays the bones
of boardwalks. While sea waves
tumble in, snow dunes ripple the coast
with crystals. Here, our vision escapes the city's bargraph
of buildings. Under a boarded down hotdog stand,
we sizzle; the white balloons of our breath hold no words.
Winter muffles the roller coaster's rails; we make
our own amusements in this skeleton-park,
abandoning ourselves to our own weather.

Stumbling back, through the merry-go-round flakes, to our room,
the shells of our ears hold an ocean sound, fingers, feet,
faces tingling like a thousand stars. Boreas bangs
on the doors. We stay up half the night, watching old movies
through the snow on TV, make love to the knock of steam.

Muriel Rogers "Dawn On The Jersey Shore"
11" x 30" Watercolor 2000 Collection of Artist Prints Available

Muriel Rogers "Surf In Loveladies"
11" x 30" Watercolor 2000 Collection of Artist Prints Available

Virginia Perle "Summer Morning, Seaside Park"
15" x 10" Watercolor 1999 Private Collection

Boardwalk Games

My youngest son and I were sitting around the living room one night, talking about the boardwalk games we used to play when he was small. Now in his thirties, Steven had spent that afternoon in one of the Seaside Heights arcades with his young nephews, and he had been regaling me with tales of road races, Western shootouts, and laser fights. Their excitement had rekindled my own, and I smiled happily as I thought about playing pinball and Skeeball alongside my sons.

"Remember all the games we used to play?" I said, a bit wistfully. "I think my favorite was the baseball game. You know, the one where, at the push of a button, a silver metal ball would rise up out of a slot in the pitcher's mound and roll down toward the batter. Remember?"

"Not really," Steven said.

"Sure," I continued. "There'd be two thumb-like plastic bats—one to the left of the plate, one to the right—that were operated by buttons on either side of the machine. You had to be ready for a curve, or a fastball, or maybe even a slider. And if you played the angle of your swing just right, you could knock the ball up a ramp and into the bleachers for a home run. Then all the painted metal runners would circle the bases while the machine loudly *kirchinged* every run that scored. It was like winning the jackpot."

"Uh-huh. And who controlled the pitches?"

"I did, usually."

"Then who operated the bats?"

"Well, me."

"So you pitched to yourself and batted against yourself, so you always knew what pitch would be coming? Where was the surprise?"

"It wasn't about surprise," I said. "And it wasn't as easy as it sounds, believe me. Getting the silver ball up the ramp took timing, it took skill..."

"I hate to tell you this, Dad, but it sounds dull."

"No, really, it was a lot of fun," I said, a little defensively. "Next time you go up to the boardwalk, you try it."

Steven smiled. "Uh... When was the last time you were in an arcade, Dad?"

"I don't know... It's been awhile. Why?"

"I hate to tell you this, but they don't have machines with silver balls and plastic bats anymore. They hardly even have *pinball* machines anymore. Those games you used to play are collectors' items now."

"No pinball?" I said, shocked.

"Well, maybe they have a few machines, but most of the games now are electronic—you know, the virtual-reality types."

"No pinball?" I repeated.

"I'm sorry, Dad. But the new games can be just as much fun. Tell you what, let's you and I both go up to the boardwalk next weekend and play a few of them. Who knows, maybe you'll find a new favorite."

"I doubt it," I mumbled. No pinball. Hrmmph.

So, on the next Saturday, Steven and I found ourselves in Lucky's Arcade on the Seaside Heights boardwalk, surrounded by children and teenagers. We exchanged a ten dollar bill for two small rolls of quarters, and Steven pointed toward something called the Off Road Challenge. Two machines sat side by side, each with a driver's seat facing a steering wheel and a huge screen.

"Why don't we start here?" he asked. "We can hook the games up so we can race each other; every time your car gets near mine, you'll see my number flash on the screen. Of course, I'll probably be too far ahead for you to worry about that."

"Eat my dust," I said. As I climbed into my seat, I remembered that Steven loved off-road racing and used to compete in mud hops in one of those four-wheel-drive vehicles where you needed practically a ladder to get to the cab. He even won a few competitions. Perhaps I had spoken too soon.

After putting in fifty cents, I checked out the brake, the gas pedal, and the small steering wheel. Nothing stuck; a good sign. The first visual on the screen offered a choice of transmissions, stick or automatic. I chose automatic. Next came a choice of vehicles. I selected the Toyota Trophy Truck; its side was pasted with sponsorship decals. Any vehicle with that many sponsors had to have something going for it.

Now both Steven and I had to choose which track we wanted: Vegas (advanced), El Paso (intermediate), or Baja (beginner). Silly me, I suggested intermediate. (I later found out that, on the beginner track, the truck didn't spin out as much, while on the Vegas track the vehicle handled much more responsively; if I barely touched the wheel, the truck would run off the road.) We also had a choice of vantage points for the race: helicopter, bumper, or behind-the-wheel. So many choices and only a few seconds to decide. We both chose a behind-the-wheel view.

With that final decision made, I adjusted myself in the seat and pressed "start," expecting the car to jump away. Instead, it just sat there. Steven leaned over. "You've got to step on the pedal, Dad."

Turning only slightly red, I pressed the pedal to the floor and the truck *vroommed* away from the starting line. Immediately, my computerized competitors jumped ahead of me. I struggled to catch up, speeding along a track that cut through the desert, but all I passed were cactuses and coyotes. On the straight part of the track, I did fine, but as soon as I hit a curve I sped off the road, smashing into the cactuses and bumping over desert shrubs, before finding myself back on the

Dick LaBonté "The Coaster"
20" x 24" Acrylic 1999 Collection of Mr. and Mrs. Bruce F. Wesson Prints Available

road again.

A few yards ahead, a pack of coyotes began crossing the road. Animal lover that I am, I slowed until they had all crossed, but even so I just missed them by inches. I looked over at Steven's screen just as he hit one. The animal broke in half, and blood gushed everywhere. I cringed. It's only a game, I reminded myself, it's only a game. I turned back to my screen, just in time to see myself heading toward a bunch of steel drums and crates at a construction site. I winced. *Crash*. The crates and drums flew like an exploding star, and then I was off the track again, bumping along.

Suddenly, the scene changed: I was heading into an abandoned mine with tram cars, supports, and forgotten skeletons. What in the world happened to the desert? I smashed into a skeleton, and the white bones flew into the dark. Before I could catch my breath, I ran into a wooden mine support that splintered into hundreds of pieces. I just missed a tram car—and then I was out of the dark night of the mine and back in the desert light, bumping back onto the track. More coyotes! Just missed! More steel drums and boxes! *Boom*! In my peripheral vision, the terrain whizzed by as I bounced over the hills and crashed into cactuses, tumbled back onto the road, and then sped straight-away toward the grandstand and the finish line, a king-sized green banner over it. Cars ahead of me screeched and skidded to a halt. My car slid sideways, stopping inches before the near pileup. Race over. I let out a long breath.

We checked our results. Steven had finished seventh. I had finished eighth. The computer cars had finished first through sixth. I longed for the days of silver balls and plastic bats.

We wandered around Lucky's for a few minutes. Then, near the back of the arcade, I spotted a game that piqued my interest. STF (Special Tactical Force) had a large eye-level screen and a separate stand that housed a gray, plastic submachine gun. The stand also had a big silver pedal at its base—much bigger than the one I had been using in the off-road race. A sticker under the screen described the Special Tactical Force and how well trained it was. Another label issued a warning: "Lifelike. Violence. Strong." Was this anything like the movie ratings PG-13, R, and the dreaded X?

Before I could walk away, a deep, somber voice emanated from the machine, informing me that a terrorist group named URDA had taken over Dry Creek Plaza. The terrorists were in the Garland Tech Center, the mall, and the plaza itself. As the voice spoke, the various terrorists and the occupied sites flashed on the screen; occasionally, the head terrorist would interrupt with a maniacal laugh. My mission, a dangerous one, would be to help liberate Dry Creek Plaza. How could I resist? Here was an opportunity to save the world, or at least one small area of it. Besides, my shooting couldn't be any worse than my driving. I put in two quarters.

The background story once again flashed across the screen, as did instructions. The pedal, I learned, controlled a protective shield with a narrow, rectangular window; this shield would protect me from most of the terrorists' attacks. However, if I wanted to fire my machine gun, I would have to lower the shield and expose myself. Ah, well; no one ever said saving humanity would be easy.

The next screen displayed three crisis sites where the enemy had established a stronghold. I pointed my gun at the one I chose to enter, the Garland Tech Center, and fired. Accompanied by the Special Tactical Force and protected by my shield, I easily got through the front door of the high glassy building. No sooner had I entered the lobby, however, than I was confronted by the enemy: tall, muscular figures with helmets and body armor, jumping out from behind

Dick LaBonté "Low Tide"
20" x 24" Acrylic 1981 Collection of Mr. and Mrs. George H. Sands Prints Available

pillars, chairs, sofas, and a desk. Red circles began appearing on the screen—a sign that they were firing at me.

I pressed my pedal, and my protective black shield came down. I fired at one figure as he leapt from behind a pillar—*pop pop pop pop*. Down he went, but two more sprang out from behind the desk and another pillar, firing. I released the pedal to raise the shield. *Ping ping ping*—the bullets bounced off harmlessly. Through the small window, I saw them run behind a pillar. I lowered the shield and fired. Holes appeared in the pillar and a terrorist fell out from behind it, bleeding. I shot until he was still, then quickly turned my gun at another terrorist as he jumped out from behind the desk. *Pop pop pop pop*. He flew to the side as I riddled the desk with bullet holes.

Suddenly, I began moving forward—or at least the screen made it seem as if I were moving. I advanced toward an open door that led into a corridor, where glass partitions looked into office suites. Now the terrorists began swarming. A burst from my gun and I heard *oh*'s and *ooh*'s as they fell back. The partitions shattered, shards flew. I stopped to raise my shield, which automatically reloaded the gun. But then a grenade from a launcher pierced the shield. Everything turned red. Game over. I had twenty seconds to decide if I wanted to continue. I did.

I was in a room with videos now. I fired at anyone that moved, and at whatever he jumped behind. They were no longer men or terrorists to me, just targets to hit as rapidly as possible. I was quick and accurate, but the figures kept coming like the clowns in the circus from their little car. Explosion, fire, smoke. Game over. I decided I had had enough and I let my twenty seconds lapse.

"It was the guy with the bazooka who got you," Steven said. "It's tough to compete with a bazooka."

That did little to console me, though. So far these electronic games had had me driving like a maniac or killing like a madman, and in neither had I felt as if I had any control over my destiny. The machine, it seemed, would always win. Not like the baseball game.

Steven and I walked around a bit, Steven pointing out a few games we might try, me shaking my head no. Then, on the far side of the arcade, I saw the mother of all boardwalk games: a bank of about seven Skeeball alleys, with each scoreboard's series of plastic-rimmed, progressively smaller half circles—10, 20, 30, 40, 50 points—gently angled against the wall. My heart danced.

"Come on!" I shouted, taking Steven's arm. Running over, I placed a quarter in the slot. Nine wooden balls automatically rumbled down a grooved runway and came to rest with a satisfying series of gentle clunks. I picked up one of the balls; it felt solid in my palm, with a pleasing heft, and its surface bore the nicks and scratches from years of use. I paused in wonder at the thousands of people who had held this ball.

Gently, I rolled the ball down the alley and listened to its diminutive sound of wood rolling on wood, set against the sound of the sea's dull roar. The ball leapt off the upturned slope and into one of the outer circles. The scoreboard registered 30 points. The next two just missed the top half-circle—50 points—and bounced over the plastic rims into the no-points catch-all at the bottom of the target. A couple of more throws netted two 30s. Then another 10, a 40, and two 20s—180 points. A few tickets spit out near the coin slot, and I quickly inserted another quarter.

The remainder of our change slowly disappeared as Steven and I rolled one wooden ball after another down the alley. Every once in a while, a ball would jump into the small hole worth 50 points, and I'd give a little shout: "Yes!" But when I tried to find that singular groove again, the ball would bounce off the plastic rims. Don't think, I kept reminding myself. Just roll. I looked over at Steven; he was just as intent, his arm swinging methodically.

Even though we were managing only mediocre scores, the red tickets began to coil at our feet. With each game we played, the ticket-snakes grew longer. After about seven games apiece, Steven and I called it quits. We tore off the tickets—each line of which by then had grown to about eight feet—and folded them accordion-style into one stack. I smiled. Although it didn't have the razzle-dazzle, shoot-'em-up, run-'em-down effects of the other video games, there was still something pleasing about this time-worn game that, like a benevolent uncle, slipped you a reward for your efforts.

Steven and I decided to save our tickets for another day, and we stepped out onto the boardwalk. The day was still bright, and the rough surf flashed with sun. We walked over to the railing and stared out at the breakers.

"I had forgotten how much fun Skeeball could be," Steven said. "Remember, when I was a kid, I used to play it all the time and dream about winning enough tickets to get the two-wheeler bike. I think you finally bought me one, so I wouldn't be spending most of my allowance at the arcade."

"I had forgotten about that," I said. "So, what do you think about the arcade games now, Mr. Virtual Reality?"

"Oh, I still like the new games. But Skeeball was like seeing an old friend. And sometimes the oldest friends are the best."

I couldn't have agreed more.

Ludlow Thorston "Summer Vacation"
2 1/2" x 9" Watercolor 1987 Collection of Artist

Virginia Perle "Island Beach Autumn"
11" x 17" Watercolor 1997 Collection of Artist Prints Available

Virginia Perle "The Wheelhouse"
8" x 13" Watercolor 1998
Collection of Artist Prints Available

Island Beach State Park

Freed from the classroom routines of the school day, my fourth graders are beaming as the yellow bus arcs across the bridge over Barnegat Bay and onto Pelican Island. There, a causeway guides us into Seaside Heights, and from there it's only a few minutes south—and a world away—to our final destination: Island Beach State Park.

Once we enter the park, I feel as if I've gone back to an earlier time—before the proliferation of houses, before telephone poles and electric wires. On Island Beach, I am taken back to the elemental world of sand, ocean, and sky; to a time before the fragile tracks of herring gulls were replaced by the hard soles of sneakers and sandals. Today I hope to share that experience with my fourth-grade class. We head toward the park's Nature Center, where a guide awaits to explain the mysteries of this ten-mile-long strip of sand, natural growth, and untold stories.

The bus driver pulls into the parking lot at the Ocean Bathing Area, where the students file off, laughing and jostling each other and generally having a good time. The bus departs, and the mothers who have come along round up all the students into a single row. Only then do I realize that the Nature Center is nowhere to be seen. The lot is deserted—no people, no cars—and the rest rooms are locked. I tell my fourth-graders to wait by some nearby benches while I walk to the boardwalk and take the stairs down to the beach, where I hope to find someone who can provide directions.

I walk out toward the surf, only to find I am totally isolated. With the high dunes behind me, the pungent smell of the ocean grows stronger. Instantly, it pulls up memories of bright days spent with my cousins, building unfinished sandcastles as the tide splashed in sooner than expected. I revel in that feeling for a moment—I was probably no older than the students waiting for me now. Then a shout from the parking lot awakens me to the reality that I have to find someone to ask about the Nature Center. I look up and down the beach, seeing only wind-carved ripple after ripple, like the ribs of an old wooden ship, and in the distance a solitary fisherman, seemingly a half-inch tall. I suddenly feel as if I were no bigger than a grain of sand. The ocean sparkles like a thousand tears, and the sky is as clear as a gull's cry. Reluctantly, I turn around and head toward the lot.

Fortunately, one of the mothers has brought along a cell phone. She pulls it from her pocketbook, and in a few minutes we are connected to the mainland again. Five minutes later, another school bus that was parked at the Nature Center picks us up and delivers us to our proper destination. While I would normally think of a cell phone as totally alien to Island Beach, today I am glad for this intrusion of technology.

Inside the center, we gather before a mural cross section of the barrier island. With the students seated around her on the floor, our guide, Christine, explains the island's different areas. She begins with the primary dunes on the ocean side, noting that they protect the island from the ocean waves. "What keeps all that loose sand in place?" she asks.

Little Christina raises her hand. "Grass?" she says.

"Yes—beach grass. Not many plants can survive the ocean's harsh salt spray. The seaside goldenrod that grows there provides food for our only migrating insect. Who can tell me what that is?" Christine looks at Ronnie's name tag and calls on him.

"The monarch," Ronnie responds.

"That's right—it migrates all the way to Mexico. Now, in addition to the primary dunes, we also have *secondary* dunes. These dunes have some shrubs and trees that can survive the harsh salt spray: black cherry, beach plum, goldenrod, beach heather, poison ivy..." Pointing to a curved plant on the mural, she says, "See how the salt spray and wind prune and shape them?

"Now this next section," Christine continues pointing to an area behind the secondary dunes, "is thick with berry-producing shrubs, and vines—so thick, in fact, that you wouldn't be able to walk through it. But just like Br'er Rabbit was used to the briar patch, the migrating song birds and other wildlife are used to the Thicket, as we call it, and they rely on it for cover and food." She turns to the boy who's waving his raised hand. "Yes, Justin?"

"You mean even with a machete you can't get through?"

Christine laughs. "Well, it would be very difficult. This brings us to the middle of the cross section. The two-lane road you came in on is called the Edge, because of all the beautiful wildflowers that grow along the road's edge. There's yucca, Queen Anne's lace, black-eyed Susan, chicory, yarrow...just so many wonderful colors in summer and autumn. It's like a patchwork quilt. Jamie, you have a question?"

"What's yucca?"

"It's a kind of wild cactus. Yes, Bobby?"

"Who plants all those flowers?"

"People carry them in on their shoes and pants, as well as with their cars. Have you ever had burrs stick to your clothes when you walk through an empty lot?"

Over half of the hands in the class shoot up, and there's some "oh, yeah" murmurs of how the burrs stick and sometimes hurt.

"Well, it's similar to that. Without your knowing it, seeds sometimes hitch a ride on your clothes. Wherever they fall off, if it's a good place, they will grow."

Christine points to the tallest section on the mural. "The Maritime Forest that we have here is very unusual for a barrier island," she says. "There are Atlantic white cedar, pitch pine,

Virginia Perle "Boater's Row (Party Island) At Barnegat Inlet"
9" x 17" Watercolor 1998 Collection of Artist Prints Available

red cedar, American holly, willow oak, sweet bay, magnolia, southern oak—all of which are slow growing and can withstand the salt in the air."

"Wow, that's a lot of trees," Frankie pipes up.

"Yes, that's what makes it so unusual. The forest is also the oldest part of the island. Next to it we have our Freshwater Wetlands, which is where a number of birds and other animals, such as turtles and frogs and muskrats, get their fresh water. The rainwater collects and floats on top of the denser saltwater, kind of like the way oil floats on water. Large cranberries grow here, as well as royal ferns and peat moss."

"One of my favorite sections is the next one—the Tidal Marshes—because it teems with life," Christine continues. "The sun, tidewater, and grasses make it an ideal place for marine life and osprey colonies. Yes, Ashley?"

"Why is there so much life there?"

"Well, there are a lot of nutrients, tons of them, and that makes it more productive than any farmland in the country. Many animals feed, breed, and nurse their young there in the salt marsh hay and salt marsh cordgrass. Now, who can tell me what erosion is? Whitney?"

"It's when something wears away the land," Whitney answers.

"That's right, and it's a constant battle in this next section of the island, the Bayshore," Christine says. "This part, right along Barnegat Bay, has eelgrass, phragmites, and cedar trees, which protect the shoreline from erosion and flooding—but not always successfully. Later, when we take our walk, you'll see where the bay has worn away some of the shore, exposing a cedar tree's roots. If we're lucky, maybe we'll spot an egret or a heron. They nest in the trees.

"The last, but certainly not least, section of the island is S.A.V., or Submerged Aquatic Vegetation. Who knows what that means?"

A few hands go up.

"Devin?"

"Submerged means under, aquatic has to do with water, and vegetation is plants," Devin recites.

"Excellent. This area on the bay has a lot of eelgrass, widgeon grass, and sea lettuce, and the water is shallow and clear. All of this makes it a good habitat for waterbirds, fish, and shellfish."

When Christine finishes her explanation, the children are allowed to stand up, walk around, and look at a jagged shark's jaw, a horseshoe crab, baleen from a whale, a dolphin's skull, a conch, a starfish, and various shells. The children touch everything and take pictures with the cameras they brought along with them.

After a while we leave the small Nature Center, get back on the bus, and travel south on the island, until we reach two trails that form a cross section of the barrier island that was displayed on the mural. We park and head off toward a little boardwalk trail that cuts through the Thicket and toward the beach.

Between the primary and secondary dunes, Christine stops and points toward the shoreline. "Legend has it that pirates harbored their boats here, and that Captain Kidd buried his treasure on one of these islands," she says. "There are even shipwrecks under some of these dunes."

Ronnie replies, "I saw old cars on the beach after a big storm once, but never any ships."

A commotion stirs at the back of the crowd, and the air fills with shouts of "Oh, look!" and "A fox, a fox!" Within seconds, a half-dozen children are running over to the side of the boardwalk to get a better look. The fox turns tail and quickly trots off along the dunes, as Christine explains how

Ludlow Thorston "On Barnegat Bay"
5" x 13 1/2" Watercolor 1997 Collection of Artist Prints Available

Ludlow Thorston "Seaside Park"
5 1/2" x 13 1/2" Watercolor 1995 Collection of Artist

the shouts and quick movements undoubtedly frightened him. We head back along the boardwalk, the children obviously disappointed that they scared the fox away.

As we begin crossing the road toward the bus, some children spot the fox again near a red cedar, its back to us. This time they move toward him slowly and quietly, fingers pressed to their lips. The sharp face of a fox flames into view along with its bushy, white-tipped tail. A couple of the girls snap pictures. The fox in his burnished fur sits on its haunches and stares expectantly at the children for about thirty seconds.

"He's looking for a handout," Christine says. "We have a saying, though: 'If you care, don't share.' If foxes learn to come up to the road for food, they could get hit by a car. There's enough natural food on the island." The children obey, and this time I sense the fox is disappointed. It turns tail, trots off, and disappears into the underbrush. We also turn and head back to the school bus, which will take us along the Edge and back toward the world we more commonly know.

Later that month, in a few of the field guides the children have written, the red fox appears again in several photos. "That was the best part of the trip" echoes from journal to journal. I have to smile; that's Island Beach State Park, where a solitary red fox can color the imagination with one look. I, however, have my own favorite moment from the trip: when I stood alone on the shore, isolated, surrounded by nothing but ridges of sand, sharp-blue sky, and breakers that thundered and rolled, just as they have for millions of years. That, too, is Island Beach State Park—and long may it be so.

The Shell

Between seaweeded crab bones and dead wood
in the ribs of the sand, I found a shell
shaped by the ocean and echoing shore.
My beachcombing fingers swirled over the contours
of its prickly points. I marveled at how
many tides filled its hollows as I listened
to its spiraled wisdom. Blessed in summer's
sun, my skin turned ripple dark, but my mind
grew white with wonder at how many men had died,
bare as this shell, on an abandoned beach,
their bones dry as wind-blown sand, their astonished
cries rung with the sea, and as deep as the shell's empty roar.
Salt marks the rocks. Seals bark and shine in the sun.
At night, hollow gongs of buoys haunt the waves.

Beverly Golembeski "Charlie's Place – Close Up"
11" x 17" Watercolor 1999 Collection of Artist Prints Available

Joyce Lawrence "Tucker's Island Lighthouse"
24" x 36" Oil 1997 Collection of Mr. and Mrs. Clark Messec Prints Available

CHAPTER 3

Dennis Foy "GSP 74.0"
10" x 12" Oil on Board 2000 Private Collection Prints Available

Dede Esenlohr "Summer Dune – August"
22" x 32" Acrylic 1995 Collection of Michael Murphy

Dede Esenlohr
"Dune Fences And Sea Grasses"
24" x 36" Acrylic 1997
Collection of A. Swords

Dede Esenlohr "Morning Walk – Past Broken Jetty"
22" x 36" Acrylic 1994 Collection of Mary Ann Smith

Dede Esenlohr
"Windswept Dune"
24" x 40" Acrylic 1998
Collection of D. Wall

Virginia Perle "Morning Light"
15" x 22" Watercolor 1996 Private Collection

A Walk In Pine Beach

Speeding on a strip of road through thriving wetlands, the car's air conditioner on max and the speakers trembling with Wagner's *Entrance of the Gods*, I turn to my wife and ask if she's spotted any wildlife.

"How can I see anything with you driving sixty-five?" she answers with a laugh.

In a blink, I realize the foolish context of the question: trapped by the creature comforts of my car, I couldn't be further removed from the nature I sought to experience. I laugh at myself and slow down for the remainder of the ride home. But later that afternoon, when I sit down to watch television, that feeling of removal returns, only more deeply. Over the past several months, more and more of my free time has been spent watching television or a video—nature programs, comedies, travel documentaries about Rome, Athens, the Far East. These armchair travels have allowed me to experience places I would never see otherwise, but they've also contracted my world in insidious ways. Sitting there as the opening credits roll, I realize that I had come to appreciate the taped and filmed versions of reality more than the real: the two-dimensional sunset on the TV river; the woods and animals with good color but no touch, smell, or depth to them; the TV programmer's sense of history rather than my own. I lived in the cave of my house watching the shadows of the real world flicker by me on the screen. That night, I resolve to not watch TV or the newly released movie fresh from the video store. It was time for a change. It was time for a walk.

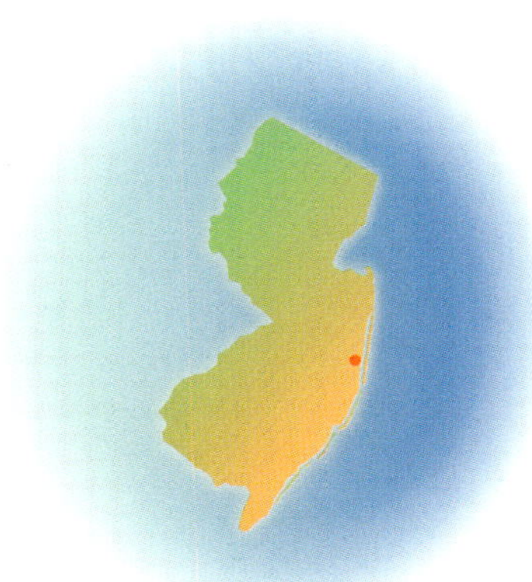

Around sunset, I leave my house and amble down to the beach across Riverside Drive. Orange, red, and yellow hues shred the sky to the west, while the river blazes with the fire of the descending sun. The windows of the houses across the Toms River are spellbinding, each with their needlepoints of reflected light; they echo the first stars appearing in the indigo eastern sky. I recall the Little Prince who loved sunsets and once watched forty-four of them just by moving his chair a few steps on his small asteroid. I will settle for just this one: sunset here is as beautiful as anywhere in the world. Soon I will be able to stand on the bank of the river, look upstream, and see the last remaining daylight, then look downstream and see the approaching night. I am in true twilight and can now feel where the word comes from: two lights, uncertain light. I stand on the shore in that subtle blending of the two.

A heavy, sweet odor of honeysuckle, which grows wild on this narrow river beach, fills the air as the earth cools. I remember once in midwinter when I entered my house and smelled this same scent; I thought my brain was playing tricks on me. Then my wife told me about her new perfume. I wonder what other scents that manufacturers might bottle—is there a market for freshly mown grass or autumn leaves? Will anyone ever need to smell the real thing again? Standing on the riverbank, I hope the answer will always be yes.

The sun sinks below plumes of tall reeds, their silvery tassels silhouetted against the last light. I half-climb, half-run up a short rabbithole-like slope, through a tangle of beach plum and bayberry bushes, and onto Riverside Drive. The town has few sidewalks, so I stay near the curb of the serpentine road. This place has not yet lost its small-town quality to the overdevelopment that has swallowed other towns nearby. In this day of malls and mini-malls, I relish the rusticity of few sidewalks and lampposts; it allows me to better see the wildflowers and stars.

Within only a few blocks, I come to one of the town's most historic structures: Admiral Farragut Naval Academy, a four-storied, bracket-shaped, wooden building with a mansard roof and two adjoining wings. Standing on what once was the site of an American Indian village, this once-elegant, Tudor-style building served as the Pine Beach Inn in 1910. People came from as far away as Pittsburgh and Texas during the height of its popularity. It became a naval academy in 1933; its students included the first American in space, Alan B. Shepard, Jr., who spent a year at the academy (1941) between graduating from high school and entering the U.S. Naval Academy. Thirty years later, Shepard became one of the few men to set foot on the moon. As a member of the Apollo 14 mission, he spent over thirty-three hours on the lunar surface—a record—and also took the first lunar golf shots, using a six-iron to drive, one-handed, two golf balls toward the stars.

In the deepening dark, the full moon begins its rise above the hollow-eyed academy. On the moon—no water, no wind, no weather—Shepard's prints remain there, a quarter of a million miles away. His academy legacy will be less enduring. Admiral Farragut, which went bankrupt in 1992, has been boarded up and sold; it will eventually be torn down and replaced with assisted living quarters, although much of the land around it will be kept as a park. I stand in awe of the lost history of this place: the old Indian village, the Inn, the Academy, and, above it all, the moon. There should be a sign: *Alan Shepard studied here. He aimed for the moon and made it.*

A brief light, then another, brings my attention closer to earth. On the spacious lawn in front of the ruined school, fireflies spangle the grass—a fleeting graffiti. I have never seen so many. Flashing. Now here. Glowing. Now there. A silent light show, no tickets needed. Even if no one witnesses it, the show will be repeated tomorrow evening. The Japanese once thought fireflies were transformed from decaying grasses. They even had firefly festivals each year in Kyoto. The city may have its neon lights, but they pale before this flickering lawn.

I continue down the street, following the lampposts and

Ludlow Thorston "Evening Sail On The Toms River"
5 3/4" x 14 1/2" Watercolor 1998 Collection of Artist Prints Available

Ludlow Thorston "Island Heights Afternoon"
5 1/2" x 11" Watercolor 1999 Collection of Artist Prints Available

their cones of light, passing under elms that loom larger at night. During the day, these trees are in our world. But at night we are in theirs, and their dark, leafy presence grows in stature. In their rooted owl-rings of age, they seem wise in ways that we will never be. Under their boughs I feel protected, and I absorb from them a sense of strength. Through their storied branches of leaves, I peer at stars and view the past from the present—the only time machine I will ever know. Do any of these stars still burn out there?

I turn left onto a sidestreet, away from the nearly dark river. I have not taken this particular route in over a year, and already I can see changes. Four of the once-wooded lots now have houses on them. They seem to have burst into being, the debris of their cocoons still strewn around their foundations: half-empty cement bags, warped two-by-fours, stray roof shingles, and torn tarpaper. I realize that, despite its still-rustic feel, Pine Beach is also undergoing the inevitable changes of modern development. There are still a few empty lots left, but these have been cleared of most of their wildness; the trees, the vines, and the tall weeds are gone. "For Sale" signs now spring up among the wildflowers.

My short, circuitous walk takes me to Station Avenue, a block away from Riverside. I recall an older friend who lived here, who I once worked with on a summer job. While in a meadow digging postholes for a sign, he told me how back in the '50s he was digging a well in his backyard when he discovered lumps of coal and corroded spikes. His curiosity drove him to research the area, and to his surprise he found that, back in the late 1800s and early 1900s, a shuttle steam locomotive rumbled down his street in Pine Beach and crossed a railroad trestle over the Toms River. The trestle had a manually operated swing bridge to allow boats to pass through. The trestle is gone, except for parts of the structure that remain underwater. Only the name Station Avenue remains, derailed from its historical source.

I walk down Station until I again come to the beach. Where the trestle once crossed the river, a narrow dock extends about twenty yards out over the water. Beside it lay concrete storm drain pipes. I think back to the new houses, freshly sprung on cleared lots, and to the naval academy with its rich history and canceled future. Looking out to where I imagined the old steam locomotive once ran, I wonder what will remain in the years to come. Will the new houses survive through the years or will they be abandoned for the weeds and wildflowers to reclaim? Will all of our efforts to tame nature—to keep it at a distance—ultimately fail? Not having a time machine, I can't tell. All I know is I must take these walks more frequently, and not forget.

I plod my way through the sand and up onto the dock. Near its end, I spot the outline of what looks like a bushy-tailed tomcat. I approach slowly. As the beams from a car turning onto Riverside sweep over us, we both freeze. Raccoon. Human. We stare at each other for about twenty seconds. Then, to my relief, the bandit I once caught rifling through my garbage waddles by me with a growl. I step aside and watch, as it disappears into the dark underbrush by the road. I, too, make my way home, back to the moth-beaten porch light my wife left on for me.

Ludlow Thorston "Pavilion"
5" x 11 1/2" Watercolor 1991 Collection of Artist Prints Available

Theresa Troise Heidel "Sudden Snow Shower"
10" x 14" Watercolor 1998

New Year's Eve, 1969

The first time that Barb and I saw the house where we would eventually spend seventeen years of our life, it was a cold, moonlit New Year's Eve. The year was 1969, and we had been invited to a party in a little town called Pine Beach. Two old friends, Harriet and John, had moved there a few months earlier, and though only forty-five minutes south of our Bradley Beach apartment, it had seemed a world away—nestled on the fringes of the Pine Barrens in Ocean County, far from the lights and action of the Northern Shore.

"Do we really want to go all the way down there on New Year's Eve?" Barb had asked. "I thought we were going to spend the night alone together. Plus, you know how crowds can affect me." I did indeed: even when Barb recognized everyone in the room, any crowd of more than four or five people could make her claustrophobic and induce a panic attack. Still, we had not seen these friends for over a year, and we had not wanted to disappoint them. Ultimately, we accepted—and I was forever glad we did.

During the drive down, Barb and I agreed on a simple signal—a tug on her earring—if she started to feel panicked. "And if that doesn't work, scream and run for the door," I said, trying not to laugh. Barb just gave me one of her best drop-dead looks. "Besides," I said, "there probably won't be very many people there."

I was wrong. By the time we arrived, the few parking spaces available had been filled; several cars had even crammed onto the front lawn. Part of the problem was the house's location: it sat opposite the Toms River on a curved two-lane road (appropriately called Riverside Drive). Anyone who didn't come early enough to grab one of the few spaces in the driveway—or to park at an angle on the front lawn—had to go to a side street perpendicular to the river.

"Certainly seems like a lot of people," Barb said as we passed the jammed driveway. I noticed she was beginning to get that deer-caught-in-the-headlights look.

"I'm right here," I said. "Remember, when we get inside, just tug on your ear and I'll come to get you."

We parked one street in and a few blocks away. Walking back along Riverside Drive, we could hear the *slap slap* of the water lapping the bulkhead and feel the icicle-sharp wind off the river. The tall, dark pines along the road swayed like reeds in the moonlight. There were no sidewalks, so we stuck close to the front yards of the well-spaced houses. The neighborhood's peacefulness seemed to calm Barb. Holding hands, we marveled at the full moon's wavery reflection on the river, and how only a few twinkles of light could be seen on the tree-lined opposite shore; the night here seemed to be darker and colder than the one we had left in Bradley Beach. As we neared the house, Barb remarked in a puff of white words how the air smelled like snow. I was glad that we were heading somewhere warm and bright.

Finally, we arrived. Tucked behind porch-high bushes and fifteen feet in from the road, the two-story house had red cedar shakes and white trim. On one side, a white stone chimney rose above it like some mysterious monument shining in the moonlight. As we stepped onto the enclosed wooden porch and up to the front door, I gave Barb's hand a gentle squeeze and a quick kiss. She took a deep breath and rang the bell.

When the door opened, a burst of light, warmth, music, and laughter rushed out to envelop us. Harriet, our hostess, greeted us each with a hug. "It's so wonderful to see you both again," she said. "I'm so glad you made the trip down."

"So are we," I said. "It's a beautiful area around here—almost serene."

Harriet smiled. "John and I love it," she said, "especially being so close to the river."

We stepped into the living room, a long, narrow area divided evenly by the path to the dining room doorway and filled with people. On one side of the room, several women from Barb's yoga class chatted in front of an upright piano. On the other, several men stood in front of the burning fireplace. I recognized one of them, a bearded young man in his twenties named David, who was an artist and lived up north. Other guests sat clustered on the sofa and chairs, or stood in groups of three or four. John leaned against the newell post of the stairway, looking down at a woman with long brown hair who sat on the steps, her arms hugging her knees. From them I could hear bits of conversation—"moon landing"...."My God, can you believe it?"...."One giant leap is right..."

"Come on," Harriet said, taking my arm and leading us toward the rear of the house. She directed us to a downstairs bedroom off to our right, just before the dining room. "Throw your coats in there," she said, "then I'll lead you to the food and wine."

As we added to the growing hill of coats on the bed, a beautiful calico cat entered the room, looked up at us for a couple of seconds, turned tail, and scooted under the bed. "Who's that?" Barb asked.

"Oh, that's Callie. We've had her for years. Crowds spook her." A little like Barb, I thought to myself. Then we were off again, Harriet leading the way. "Come on, I'll give you a quick tour of the house," she said.

As promised, Harriet first took us to the dining room, where more guests had stationed themselves around a table heaped with cold cuts, salads, hot pasta dishes, and assorted condiments. On a waist-high island that separated the dining area from the kitchen, three bottles of wine—red, white, and rose—stood opened and waiting.

"I'm still not satisfied with the windows in here," she said, pointing to a row of three rectangular panes along the top of the outside wall. "I want to lower them so the sun will fill the room each morning, and I can have a view of the river."

Pouring myself a glass of red wine, I stepped into the kitchen. The window above the sink had two shelves filled with plants, African violets. Harriet followed me. "We have to put a new floor in here," she said, looking down at the wooden floorboards that had thin spaces between them. Off to the right, she pointed to a porch that she had recently remodeled into a TV room and laundry room. The room had many windows and a door that led into the backyard.

"It's a little too cold during the winter, but in the summer that room gets a wonderful breeze," she said. "Now, come, I want to show you both the remodeled bathroom upstairs." She led us back through the dining room and out toward the throng of guests. On our way, I noted that the downstairs bathroom had a large, deep cast-iron bathtub with lion's paws. I saw Barb's eyes light up with visions of long bubble baths; the tub we had at home was rather cramped.

As we started up the wooden stairs, the first thing I noticed was a picture of the full moon caught in the branches of pine needle sprays. What a fascinating painting, I thought—until I realized it was actually a narrow window at the top of the landing. Barb, looking at the same view, must have had a similar perception. "It's a window!" she exclaimed.

"Yes," Harriet said, obviously used to such comments. "It's one of my favorite windows to look out and watch the weather."

The upstairs had two bedrooms: one that overlooked the backyard and a huge locust tree, and a smaller one that faced the river. Harriet skimmed over them and ushered us into her newly remodeled bathroom, which had a bathtub near two windows that looked out onto the branches of the locust. The room also contained a separate shower stall and a large vanity topped with a theatrical-bulb mirror. Then the doorbell rang. "You two feel free to look around," Harriet said, heading back toward the steps. "I've got to see to my guests."

We poked around a bit more, then decided to go back downstairs. But first we stopped on the landing in front of the window. Gazing out at the moon, Barb said, "You know, there's a circle around it. I still think it's going to snow."

I nuzzled her warm, perfumed neck. "Maybe, but let's go down and enjoy the party." Turning around to me, she said, "Wait. I need a hug before you push me off into the crowd."

Once downstairs, Barb and I heaped our plates full of meats and salads, then re-emerged into the crowded living room. "Mingle, mingle," Barb said stoically as she went off toward the women from her yoga class. I headed toward the group by the fireplace. As I approached, I realized they were talking about the war in Vietnam. The one I recognized, David, had escaped the draft with a punctured eardrum. He was describing the protest he had taken part in recently in Washington.

"I've never seen so many people," he said. "How could Tricky Dick deny the will of so many Americans? How can he continue this horrible war?" Behind him an ash fell onto the grate as the firewood crackled and popped. Between the spaces of their conversation, I heard the flames fluttering. When I realized I was paying more attention to the flames than to David, I decided to move off to a less depressing conversation.

In the dining room, I saw John standing with a few older men who were extolling Neil Armstrong's walk on the moon. "Surely, this is the greatest event of the decade, if not the century," said one man in a soft-spoken tone.

"Yeah," said John, "it's one of those happenings that

people years from now will want to know where you were when it took place."

I was about to toss in a comment about how the poets might view the moon now when someone grabbed my arm, and I turned to see Barb with a wide-eyed, eager expression. "Excuse me, fellows, I have to show Frank something," she said, leading me back toward the living room.

"Are you OK?" I asked as Barb hurried me through the doorway. I looked for the tell-tale signs of encroaching panic.

"Yes, yes, but you have to see this," she said, taking my plate and putting it on a nearby telephone table. Bringing me to the staircase, she turned off the light at the top of the landing and switched on the outside floodlight. " Look!" she exclaimed.

I did, and my jaw dropped. The pine branches that only an hour ago had been entangled in moonlight were now clumped with snow. In the floodlight I could see the flakes swirling like a swarm of white bees. Behind us, the party continued in full swing—clinking glasses, loud talk, laughter, and a bluesy Janis Joplin song, *Me And Bobby McGee*, winding its melody through the house.

Barb and I looked at each other, and in that moment the same thought hit. Quietly, we turned off the floodlight and snuck into the bedroom to dig out our coats. Within a minute we were standing once again on the enclosed porch. The wind had let up a bit, but the snow—silent, soft, and slow—continued to fall heavily. Standing shoulder to shoulder, we gazed at the flakes descending and dissolving into the timeless black river across the street.

On the hushed porch, the secret of the snow all around us and the muffled din of the party inside, Barb whispered, "Someday we'll have a house like this by the water to share with our friends and family."

"We can dream, can't we?" I whispered back. I took her hand, and we went into the snowfall, crunching along the lawn until we stood next to the pine that had lured us out here. I looked at Barb; her wild red hair had taken the shape of the wind, and her arms stretched up toward the night sky as if in welcome. There was no chance of a panic attack now.

"Amazing," I said. "It's New Year's Eve, in less than an hour a new decade will start, and all I want to do is remain in this moment with you forever."

Barb came over and put her arms around me. "As long as we're together, it won't end; it will just keep on getting better."

Far off, some people laughed, Janis sang, the world went on. I didn't care. A magical cocoon of snow spun itself around the house, around us, drawing us into each other. Embracing for the second time that evening, we renewed our vows of love, secretly and silently as the snow.

Years later, after Harriet and John had moved upstate and, rather than sell the house, asked us to take care of it—yes, dreams can come true—I would sometimes walk through the house and remember that New Year's Eve party of so long ago: David by the fireplace decrying Vietnam; John in awe over the first moon landing; Harriet proudly taking us from room to room. Even as Barb and I grew into middle age, that first magic night remained as strong as ever in our memories, and it made our life there all the richer.

That was especially true on the nights it snowed, when we would go to the darkened landing and look out our favorite window. I would stand behind Barb and put my hands around her waist, and together we would stare at the floodlit pine, the madly swirling flakes, and—if we tried—two figures: a wild redhead and man with curly dark hair, both in their twenties. They would stand there, holding each other as if they'd never leave. Somehow, we knew they never would.

Ann Hayes "The Cedar Porch"
30" x 42" Watercolor 1999 Collection of Susannah DuPuy

Joyce Lawrence "First Bridge At Sunset"
17 1/2" x 24" Pastel 1998 Collection of Joe and Gloria Gartner

Canoeing Down Cedar Creek

Born under the water sign of Pisces, I am drawn to water as the sea is drawn to the moon. The motion and sound of streams, creeks, and rivers are to me as flickering campfires are to a lone camper. This may explain why, while passing Cedar Creek Campground one day and seeing two young men taking down a canoe from their car roof, I inexplicably had the urge to join them.

This impulse followed me all the way home. I couldn't understand it; I had not picked up a paddle since I was twenty and a counselor at a Fresh Air Fund camp. But while the memories of that summer had stayed with me—guiding a silver canoe on a large, dark lake, listening to the loon's cries—I hadn't set foot in a canoe since then, even though my current home in Ocean County is known for its beautiful waterways. It made me think of when I lived in New York, and how people would come from all over the world to see the Statue of Liberty and the Empire State Building—but when I went to school in Texas and people asked what they were like, I couldn't answer; I had never visited either one of them. I was determined not to let that happen again.

As soon as I got home, I called my son Alan, who had gone canoeing down Cedar Creek with his wife and kids only a week before. "How would you like to do it again, but with a new passenger?" I asked him. Ever eager to spend more time on the water—though not a Pisces, he might as well be—Alan agreed to join me, and said he would make arrangements for the coming weekend. I immediately felt lighter as twenty years of procrastination slipped off my back.

And so it was that, on a sunny Saturday morning in early August, Alan and I found ourselves heading down Route 9 toward Cedar Creek. We had just experienced the hottest July ever recorded—several times, the temperature had approached one hundred degrees, with little rain to cool things off—and this day seemed ready to offer more of the same. Already, at 9:00 A.M., the thermometer had pushed past eighty degrees. It was a good time to turn to the creek and canoeing.

At the campground, we rented a fifteen-foot aluminum Grumman for thirty bucks, stored it in the trailer attached to a van, and were transported in about twenty minutes to Double Trouble State Park. (A historical village of cedar houses that sprang up around cranberry bogs and a sawmill, Double Trouble received its name from a dam that washed out twice in one day, thus causing "double trouble" for the mill.) Our drop-off point was White Bridge, a low wooden structure only a few feet removed from the tea-colored creek. Helping us to unload our canoe, the van driver told us our pick up point would be on the left bank by an old railroad trestle about three hours downstream. After staring off toward our invisible destination, I peered over the bridge's railing—and was amazed to look down on birds flying. Long forked-tail swallows, their iridescent, steel-blue colors shining in the sun, graced the water's surface with their swift, smooth flight—an invisible calligraphy written with their long, pointy tails. The flow of the birds and the creek itself evoked lines from a favorite poem of mine, *Fern Hill* by Dylan Thomas: "*And the sabbath rang slowly / in the pebbles of the holy streams. / All the sun long it was running, it was lovely...*" Suddenly, I was very glad I had made this decision to be here with my son.

We carried the canoe down to the bank, put our paddles and water bottles into the bow, and waded into the cold current. When the canoe was out far enough to take our weight and not get caught on the pebbles and sand, we climbed aboard and donned our life jackets. Slowly, I dipped my paddle into the water. When we were renting the canoe, one of the proprietors told us that Cedar Creek was the first stream to be declared a wild and scenic river under the Wild and Scenic River Program back in 1972. She also said proudly, "It's one of the cleanest streams in the Northeast." I remembered reading about how a group of local citizens had fought to keep an adult community building from being built along its banks. Robert E. Anstett, who had then been president of Citizens Conservation Council of Ocean County, was quoted in the *Asbury Park Press* as saying, "You don't let something like this get destroyed. There's a responsibility of stewardship." Sitting in the middle of the creek now, I couldn't have agreed more.

Paddling downstream, I soon felt as if the soft sounds of the water had entered my bloodstream; my breathing seemed to slow, and a peaceful feeling washed over me. The creek snaked its way through a cool canopy of pines and cedars, and sunlight dappled the water and our canoe. I raised my head toward the sky, trying to feel the bits of sun as they fell on my face. Then, gliding around a bend, we encountered our first obstacle: a fallen tree trunk that blocked almost half of the creek. "We'll go around it," Alan said. "Lean to the left." I did—but too far. In an instant, the canoe upended and both Alan and I splashed into the cool water.

The first thing I heard after the splash was Alan laughing. I stood up—the water here was only about thigh-deep—and turned to him; he was standing with his hands holding his sides, dripping wet, a smile engulfing his face. A little embarrassed, I managed a grin. The overturned canoe winked in the sunlight and tried to float away on the slow current. We held on, dragged it ashore by a sandy place near a footbridge, and emptied it of water. Sheepishly, I asked, "Did you fall in when you went with your wife and son?"

"A number of times. Don't worry about it, Dad; half of the fun is falling in and cooling off."

We emptied the wet sand from our rubber water-shoes and

Joyce Lawrence "Marshes At Sunset"
10 1/2" x 18 1/2" Pastel 1999 Collection of Artist Prints Available

put them on again. Before getting back into the canoe, though, we walked up to the footbridge, which we discovered was part of a nature trail that extended through the park. Walking down the path a little ways, I spotted a pitcher plant with red flowers and clusters of erect, hollow, pitcher-like leaves, each with reddish-purple veins striating a white background. I said, "Alan, look at this. This is an amazing plant. It's carnivorous."

"You mean like the plant in *Little Shop of Horrors*?" Alan loved horror movies and had an offbeat sense of humor. His favorite comic strip was *The Far Side*.

"No," I said. "Carnivorous in that it eats insects. Well, it doesn't really eat them; it dissolves them. They're lured in by the colorful leaf and the nectar, fall into a pool of collected water, and are decomposed by some enzyme in the plant. Then the plant absorbs the nutrients." Alan's eyes widened as I spoke, and when I finished he shook his head. "Wow," he said softly, appreciative of the small horrors of the plant world.

As we made our way back, Alan noticed a red salamander on a plant near the bridge. About three inches long, it had short, stout legs, a tail that was thick at the base and then tapered to a point, and black spots all over its sunset-red body. Alan picked it up—it didn't seem to mind. When I touched it, the skin felt like a piece of latex, smooth and cool. Gently, Alan returned the salamander to its spot, and we headed back to the canoe.

Moving downstream once again, we soon came to the Garden State Parkway. Above us, cars whizzed along with no inkling that the purest creek in Jersey and two paddlers were gliding by under them. It made me think of all the times I had traveled that same road, paying little attention to the natural world around me—a world of which I had now become a part, and in which the speeding drivers and their cars seemed almost alien. I wondered where they were all going, and why they were in such a rush. Slowly we moved downstream, taking our time. Then our hull scraped concrete and we stopped: the shallowness of the water had forced the canoe to run aground on the Parkway's foundation. I couldn't help but laugh; once again, modern civilization had found a way to intrude. Stepping out so the canoe could become buoyant again, we walked downstream a few yards until we cleared the overpass. A few days later, while driving on the Parkway, I tried to spot the creek from my car, but couldn't see anything because of all the foliage. As if in self-protection, nature had closed the door.

As Alan and I paddled on, the sounds of the highway diminished, and nature again reasserted itself. We heard the sounds of many birds but saw only a few: a sparrow, a blue jay, a towhee. We heard frogs plopping into the creek before they even saw us. Alan spotted a turtle basking on a half-sunken log near the bank. When he paddled closer to look, the turtle disappeared underwater.

On we went, occasionally bumping into a submerged rock or tree limb. At one point, Alan and I stopped paddling and drifted a little ways. There was a dead calm in the air—no wind stirring the trees, no sounds of civilization. I put my hand into the dark, rust-colored water: it was cool, and I felt the slow, steady force of the current. A white cabbage butterfly, like a little ghost, flitted across our path. We floated along, and the creek opened into a marshland with grasses, white water lilies, and cedars. On one of the lily pads, we spotted a green frog. When it spotted us, it hopped into the creek by a branch that looked like the arm of a drowning man.

I also noticed many more dragonflies and damselflies skimming this part of the creek for food. They varied in colors—dark brown with yellow stripes, powder-blue, green,

Symon Cowles "The Meadows"
10" x 24" Oil on Wood 1999 Private Collection Prints Available

purple, black—and moved at different speeds. Some flew slowly with oversize wings; a few seemed to dance, never staying in one place too long; others hovered briefly, then jetted away. Nearby, a bug-eyed dragonfly with lacy, fishnet wings and an iridescent blue abdomen hovered motionless over the water. It was a fearsome-looking insect with its huge, staring eyes and an exposed belly that seemed almost electric. As a kid, I read that, in prehistoric times, dragonflies had wingspans of up to two feet—true miniature dragons of the sky, minus the fire-breathing. Watching this descendent before us now, a God-like stillness held us all transfixed and peaceful for a moment. Then the dragonfly darted upward and out of sight, and the creek flowed on.

Alan and I had been out on the water now for more than two hours, and were starting to tire. We began drifting more and more, letting the current propel us. I put my hand back into the water, and for a moment imagined myself connected to the Atlantic Ocean a few miles away. I felt myself sweep past the small beaches along the creek's shore, past the white yachts in the marinas on Barnegat Bay, past the tiny Sedge Islands with their myriad wildlife, and beyond the shoals of the shifting barrier islands, into the open ocean. From the seat of this aluminum canoe, I felt as if I were connected to all the Jersey Shore—to all creation, in fact. I tilted my face toward the sun and smiled.

Just as we were approaching our third hour of canoeing, the creek meandered into a horseshoe bend. Beyond rose the railroad trestle like a little castle, our pickup point. The sight injected new life into our paddle strokes. As we neared the bridge, we could see a group of five teenagers playing on the trestle, which had graffiti spray-painted on its stone foundation: love notes, names, dates, and a couple of obscenities. Bone-weary, Alan and I passed under the bridge, rolled into the creek, and waded ashore, pulling the canoe up with us. As we waited for our ride, we watched the two girls and three boys chase each other around the wooden supports, smoking and playing with empty beer cans that someone had left behind. I tried to focus on the murmuring of the creek, the play of sunlight on the surface. Finally, the van arrived, and we climbed in and headed to the campground.

Once back at our cars, we sank into the front seats. Alan started the engine and quickly turned on the air conditioning. After a few minutes of cooling down, we drove out of the campground and rejoined the traffic on Route 9, which was lined up at a light.

I sighed. "Just think, last week I was at this very spot, passing by the campground entrance and wondering what it would be like to go canoeing down Cedar Creek. Now I can finally say that I've done it."

"Congratulations, Dad. So, was it everything you had hoped?"

I smiled and let my mind meander. I thought of the forked-tail swallows and their graceful flight, and the way my paddle sounded upon first slipping into the stream. I thought of my upending the canoe, of Alan's laughter, and his wonder over the pitcher plant. I thought of the turtle sunning itself on the log, the dragonfly that hovered so magnificently before us, and the cool water rushing over my hand, connecting me to the greater world.

"More," I said. Then the light turned green and, slowly, we flowed on.

Lines For Summer

Sun fills the puddle;
nothing moves. A cicada
sizzles in the elm.

Barbara J. Cocker "Ribbons Of Blue"
48" x 36" Acrylic 1984 Collection of Barbara Beinicke

Beth Kantor "Early Snow"
36" x 28" Watercolor 1999 Private Collection

Pine Barrens Reveries

The sixth-grade students and I stared out the second-story windows of the Toms River Intermediate School, our mouths open. Toward the south, only about a dozen miles away, a wall of smoke billowed from the fire that had been raging for several days in New Jersey's famed Pine Barrens. The announcement over the intercom still hung as heavy as the smoke-smell in the air: "All after-school activities are cancelled for this afternoon. Please go straight home after dismissal."

We heard the wail of sirens in the distance. One student excitedly asked, "Do you think they'll dismiss school early?" Another girl said nervously, "It can't reach us, can it?" I didn't answer.

This was all many years ago, in the late 1960s. As it turned out, the fire didn't reach us, at least not physically. But it did give us something to think about and talk about. It had started on April 20 and was not declared out until May 1, after burning 75,925 acres of land. Fire trucks and equipment were called in from all over the state to help contain it. It was my first close encounter with a fire of that magnitude, but I later learned it's typical for the Pine Barrens to catch fire about once every six or seven years. "With those pine needles, they're a regular tinderbox in dry, windy weather," one old-timer said. The shortleaf pine and the pitch pine, which proliferate in the Barrens, are particularly suited for fires: not only does their thick bark keep the trees well insulated, but the high temperatures cause the pine cones to pop and seeds to sprout. Through the many fires over the years, these pines survived the natural selection and dominated the area.

At least they used to.

July 1969. A building boom was underway in Ocean County, and many senior citizen villages were being constructed. A young teacher in need of a summer job, I found work with one of the crews laying water pipe in Whiting. This particular area, cleared of pine, looked like a desert—hot, dry, and sandy. As we waited for a load of pipe, Kenny, our foreman, told us to break for lunch early. "The truck with the pipe should be here in an hour," he said. "Might as well eat now."

After we finished lunch, Walt, who worked the front end loader, came bouncing by on his yellow machine and stopped. "Hey, any of you guys want to see something interesting? Climb into the bucket and I'll show you," he said, his gleeful eyes looking down on us from the cab. This was unusual, because Walt usually wore a sad-eyed, stoic expression—a carryover from his days in World War II, when his job was to gather up the dead bodies on the field, put them into plastic bags, and try to identify them. He lowered the bucket so that three of us—myself and two others, Vinny and Bobby—could get in.

"Wa ja find, Walt, a dead body?" Vinny asked as we set off.

"No, you'll see," Walt said, throwing an empty brown bottle onto the sugary sand and shifting into a faster gear. After bumping along the sandy road for a while, we came upon a section of blackened pines. "This is where that big fire was," Walt yelled above the sound of the loader.

"*This* is what you brought us to see?" Bobby yelled indignantly. "A big patch of black nothing?"

"No, it's just a little ways more," Walt answered, and we bumped along. Finally, after my teeth seemed ready to loosen from my gums, Walt jerked the loader to a stop and said, "Here it is." We gazed out onto a field of bushes about five to six feet high. Jumping out of the bucket, we took a closer look and found clusters of ripe blueberries shining in the midday sun.

"My ex-wife and I used to come here," Walt said, laughing. "I had almost forgotten about this place. It used to be a farm." We eagerly started picking and eating as many berries as we could; in a few months, they too would be gone. Warm, succulent, and sweet, the berries quickly stained our lips and fingertips, but we didn't care. "Nothing like New Jersey blueberries!" I yelled. Walt, perched on the seat of his loader, looked down on us and smiled, his teeth a swath of rich, ripe purple.

On the northeastern edge of the Pine Barrens, my students and I were playing softball during lunch one afternoon when two of the boys lumbered over, carrying a huge turtle about fifteen inches long and almost as wide. It had a thick, wrinkled neck, stubby legs half-covered with warts, and a dark brown shell. The boys had discovered it under the pine needles and oak leaves in the woods bordering the field. The ballgame came to a stand-still as the awe-struck children gathered around.

"Ooh, can we keep it?" they pleaded, almost in unison.

I shook my head. "It lives here," I said. "This is its home. Would you want to be taken away from your home and your family?"

"What kind of a turtle is it?" one of the girls asked, taking off her mitt.

"It might be a snapper," I said. With that, one of the boys put a twig up by its mouth. With a quick lunge, the turtle snapped the twig in two. "Wow! It sure is!" he said.

"Put it back before someone gets hurt," I ordered. The two boys who had found the turtle took it back to the bordering

Edward J. Kojola "Heading Home From Barnegat"
10 1/4" x 14 1/4" Watercolor 1994 Collection of Artist Prints Available

Edward J. Kojola "Lifesavers"
15" x 20" Watercolor 2000
Collection of Artist

needles and leaves, and soon after we headed back to school.

Upon returning to the classroom, I sent the two boys to the library to bring back a field guide to turtles. They did, and the class confirmed the turtle we had found was indeed a snapper.

"Do you think it's back with its family now?" one girl asked.

"I'm sure of it," I said. "And I know it's very happy."

Not long after, the section where the boys had found the turtle was cleared, and another elementary school rose on that spot. In the years that followed, a community college, a few housing developments, and several strip malls sprang up along the avenue, which itself grew into a four-lane highway. All that remained of the natural growth was a patch of dark pines so tightly packed that, even on the sunniest days, the copse stood in deep shadow. Every evening I passed it on my way home from school, and the lines from Robert Frost's poem *Stopping By Woods On A Snowy Evening* always came to mind: *"The woods are lovely, dark, and deep..."*

Inevitably, I drove by one day and saw a team of workmen clearing the small patch to make way for another store. The pines were down on their sides and being converted into wood chips, which would later be carted away by a dump truck. Looking at the toppled trees, I suddenly thought of the snapper turtle. I wondered if he had found a new home long ago, or had taken up residence in the small copse and was now being evicted. Driving along, I vividly saw his wrinkled neck, wart-studded legs, and slow, sad eyes blinking in the noonday sun, wanting only to return to his natural environment. The next day I found a new route home from school.

The last sentence in John McPhee's *The Pine Barrens* reads, "At the rate of a few hundred yards or even a mile or so each year, the perimeter of the pines contracts." That was written over thirty years ago. Today, as I write this, another sizable development is going up between Route 9 and the Garden State Parkway in rustic Waretown. And so it goes.

One year, in late spring, I walked out of my house in Pine Beach and into a snowfall with large, flimsy flakes. I caught one of the flakes in my hand. It wasn't cold, and with a little pressure it crumpled, leaving a gray smudge on my palm. I looked south, and could see smoke rising from down in Lacey Township. The fires had returned to the Barrens.

Gazing up at the ash that fell around me, diminishing what had been a bright, sunny day, I remembered that time years before when fire raged for nearly two weeks. How long would the fire last this time—a day? two days? longer? It was all part of the natural cycle, in which pine cones popped and seeds spilled and new growth sprouted, phoenix-like, from the ashes of the old. Then I thought of all the new developments, strip malls, condos, and other construction that had eaten away at the edges of the Pine Barrens; how many of them might be in the path of the fires, and how many would survive? In the end, who would inherit this remarkable region?

I had a pretty good idea of the answer. The flakes of ash fell around me, as if in celebration, and the smoke billowed a few miles away. Standing there, I imagined I could hear the pines sighing as the flames approached—not in sadness, but in acceptance, as if they were saying, "Yes, this too will pass; this, too, will pass."

Patty Niebling
"At Rest Before The Race"
23" x 32" Pastel 1996
Collection of Lockhart Jones
Prints Available

Patty Niebling "Cluster Of Optimist Prams"
10" x 22" Pastel 1995 Collection of Nancy and Alfred Califano Prints Available

Paula Kolojeski "River View"
16" x 24" Pastel 1996 Private Collection Prints Available

Freeze Frame

*

Snow one star above

a field of stars

a full moon arcs

the sky by degrees

a single digit night

shadows of

pines procession

the hushed field

eons ago

still

moon

pine

star

snow

Retirement Village

I see them yellow on the hill, steel bodies
exuding oil, teeth ready to chew out
the land. Moving in, they bite the earth
down to a bare geometry, cementing
the views. I hear tracks clanking, sprockets inching
them forward. They leave behind houses in hundreds,
pencil line maples, lawns; and here, the old come
to wait like grave elephants that lumber
from the herd. At night, there are labyrinths
of walks where every corner and lawn and house
repeat, and the minotaur of age
and time snorts on some unseen street.

Carla Coutts-Miners "Light Fun"
23" x 28" Watercolor 1999 Private Collection Prints Available

CHAPTER 4

Dennis Foy "GSP 35.3"
10" x 12" Oil on Board 2000 Private Collection Prints Available

Elaine Sgambati "Day's End"
48" x 36" Oil 1987 Collection of Artist Prints Available

Elaine Sgambati "A Walk Along The Jetty"
30" x 40" Oil 1992 Collection of Artist Prints Available

Beverly Golembeski "Misty Barney"
17" x 11" Watercolor 1997 Collection of Artist Prints Available

Climbing Barnegat Lighthouse

Although it never made it onto the back of the newly minted quarter, Barnegat Lighthouse is one of the most famous landmarks of the Jersey Shore, and the only one with a nickname: "Old Barney." How does a lighthouse become a landmark *and* get a nickname? That's what I set out to discover one Saturday afternoon as my wife, Barb, and I drove over the causeway connecting Long Beach Island to the mainland.

Once on the island—in the town of Ship Bottom, to be exact—we drove north through Surf City, North Beach, Harvey Cedars, and Loveladies, passing a mix of modern, geometric-shaped homes, shingled cottages, and even a few Victorians where sea captains once slept. (Many had their own nicknames—"Sea More," "Spin Drift," "Ocean Star," and "Dune Scape" among them.) Eventually, we began seeing more and more front lawns decorated with small wooden replicas of the lighthouse, their top halves a fire-engine red and their bottoms a stark white. Some even served as mailboxes, standing about four feet tall. "Don't ask me why, but I think we're in Barnegat Light," Barb said, a grin spreading across her face.

At the northern tip of the island, where the shadow of Old Barney fell over the state park that surrounded it, I parked our car in a lot facing the inlet. Barb, preferring to watch the boats and get something to eat, stayed behind as I set off along the path to the lighthouse. A couple of fishermen walked by with poles on their shoulders and pails clanking. In the shade of a red cedar, a woman sat on a bench reading *The Perfect Storm*. Nearby, a sign announced that the area featured one of the last remnants of maritime forest in New Jersey; with its black cherry, American holly, eastern red cedar, and sassafras, it provided a handy resting place for migrating birds. The nature lover in me stirred, but right then I was more excited about seeing the lighthouse that had captured the imagination of so many people.

For some strange reason, Barb and I had not been able see the lighthouse from the road; it was as if it had been camouflaged. Now, as I came to a clearing, it suddenly loomed over me like a dinosaur of old, its girth massive and its red-and-white tower rising against the cloudless sky. Immediately, my once-intense acrophobia returned, and a wave of dizziness overcame me. I was determined to make the climb, though. I walked up to a window at the base of the tower where an obviously bored young girl sat on a stool collecting money. Without looking up, she intoned, "One dollar." I handed over a crisp bill and asked if there were any places to rest on the way up.

"Sure," she said, still looking bored. "There are seven landings; you can stop on any one of them."

Thanking her, I went inside to where the first of the lighthouse's two hundred seventeen metal steps, each painted a bright yellow, began their slow, spiraling ascent. Holding both railings, I steeled myself and forced my way to the first landing, which was actually a small room with a window looking out toward the Atlantic. The room contained several black-and-white photos, each of which supplied information about the lighthouse. One told about the original forty-five-foot-tall tower that had stood on the inlet in 1835, and that succumbed to erosion twenty years later. Another described how the present lighthouse was started in 1857 and finished about one and a half years later, in 1859. Made of brick, it stood one hundred sixty-five feet above sea level. The U.S. army engineer who supervised its construction was a graduate of West Point, Lieutenant George G. Meade. Prior to his work on Old Barney, he had completed the Absecon Lighthouse. Later, of course, he became a Civil War hero when on July 3, 1863, he defeated General Robert E. Lee at Gettysburg—a turning point for the Union forces. Impressed by Old Barney's pedigree, I continued from photo to photo, absorbing as much history as possible.

Finally, I took a deep breath and proceeded to the next landing. I refused to look up or down, instead thinking about what I had just read. When the new Barnegat Lighthouse first turned on its light, on January 6, 1859, James Buchanan was president of the United States, the great American poet Walt Whitman was forty years old, and the Civil War was still two years in the future. When the lighthouse's beacon—a three-ton Fresnel lens that stood twelve feet high and measured six feet in diameter—was made in 1856 by Henri La Paute of Paris, it would be another thirty years until France bestowed on us the Statue of Liberty. Now here I was, more than one hundred forty years later, climbing these same steps that Meade had created. So many lives.

Advancing to the third landing, I concentrated on the red brick walls of the structure; I felt a little light-headed, but as long as I focused my vision on the bricks, I would be all right. The stairs were securely grounded and, even though they weren't exactly the Yellow Brick Road, their sunshine-yellow cheered me on. Up I went, the cylindrical tower growing slightly more narrow and the landing alcoves constricting as I ascended. On the next landing, a narrow window guarded by a heavy wire cage looked out over the inlet. It was a beautiful day—sunny, 86°F, and low humidity. White boats of all sizes and shapes came and went along the water, each leaving behind them a V-shaped wake. It looked like a playground for boaters—even though Barnegat Inlet was one of the most dangerous on the Jersey Coast because of its fast currents, shifting sandbars, and offshore shoals. But the record shows that a lot fewer shipwrecks occurred by the Barnegat shoals after the light went into operation; the Fresnel lens could be

Dede Esenlohr "Barnegat Sails"
15" x 26" Acrylic 1997 Collection of L. Harkrader

seen almost twenty-five miles at sea. The clang of footsteps from people below broke my reverie, and I continued my climb.

The landings now were very limited in space. The windows had been replaced with yellow portholes—cones, really, whose diameter tapered as they progressed to the outer hull of the tower. This high up, I was feeling a little woozy and began moving more slowly. But I was almost at the top. Voices above me grew louder, until at last I reached the gallery; a few more steps led to the room from which the Fresnel lens had sent out its beam for so many years, but a thin chain and a small sign prohibited anyone from going up there. In the gallery, a red, wooden door with heavy green hinges led to an outside observation deck. The door reminded me of something from *Alice In Wonderland*, and I wondered what would happen if I stepped through; would I enter into an enchanted land? Deciding to find out, I exited the gallery—and immediately found myself surrounded by pale sky, above everything except a one-engine plane pulling a banner about Budweiser beer. I felt no fear of heights here, where thick red bars ran above and before me, keeping me from empty air and long plunges. I felt only exhilaration.

Looking down on the east side, I saw long jetties running the length of the inlet, like gray teeth in a jaw. People about three inches tall stood on the boulders, fishing or just gazing at the horizon. Beyond each jetty, the darker blue of the ocean ran toward and ultimately blended into the lighter shade of the sky. A few feet from me, a little boy and girl stood beside their mother and shouted down, "Hi, Grandma! Hi, Grandpa! Up here!" Below, two three-inch-tall people with gray hair looked and waved. The mother laughed. On the south side, I saw the maritime forest treetops, the black-tarred roofs, and the parking lot where cars' shiny hoods needled back the sunlight. I looked down Long Beach Island, its thin, smooth edge facing the ocean, its rough edge bordering the bay. Water towers, like golf balls on tees, lined the island as far as the eye could see, each appearing smaller and less distinct with distance. I almost expected some giant golfer to come and take a practice swing. But not even a cloud passed.

Circling to the northwest, the Oyster Creek power plant's smokestack in Forked River rose like a thin stem without a flower. Below me, white boats—motorboats, yachts, sailboats—still came and went, their motors growling and their hulls smacking the waves. The mosquito sounds of the jet skis flitted in and out. I thought of the sailing ships for which this lighthouse was built, and of how things had changed. Then, taking a last look around—the RV campers on the end of Island Beach State Park, across the inlet; the white back of a tern against the green waters; a red buoy bobbing merrily near the sandbar; Barb waving by the park's gift shop—I went back through the arched red door. Clutching the railing, I cautiously began descending the spiral stairs. That light-headed feeling washed over me again, but I told myself not to look down. At the next alcove, I stopped and felt the red bricks. They were cool, smooth, and solid, just like this lighthouse. I wondered how sailors must have felt, seeing this solid brick tower, the lens like a candle in the window.

Down I went, from landing to landing, concentrating on each step. As I approached the bottom of the stairway, I couldn't resist: like Lot's wife, I decided to look up. While I did not turn into a pillar of salt, I was stunned by the beauty of the lighthouse's interior dimensions. I felt as though I were in a chambered nautilus, where each chamber was a perfect scale model of the one before, only larger and slightly rotated. The red of the brick and the yellow stairs only enhanced the beauty. Something in me wished that George Meade were here

Carol Freas "Crabbers"
6 1/2" x 15 1/4" Watercolor 1997 Collection of Artist Prints Available

Carol Freas "Inlet Deli, Barnegat Light"
5 3/4" x 15 1/2" Watercolor 1996 Collection of Artist Prints Available

with me to share this vision.

Leaving, I saw the young girl who had collected my fee, still in her little room. She appeared more bored than ever when I last left her, her head down on her folded arms. Passing, I said, "That was the best dollar I've spent in a long time." She looked up and smiled wanly.

After meeting Barb at the gift shop, we went to the Dairy Queen across the way, where Barb ordered a Mud Slide to compensate for the greenhead flies that had bitten her while she waited. As she licked at some melting ice cream, she asked, "So, did you successfully find out why Old Barney is a landmark?"

I thought of Meade, of the two children shouting to their grandparents, of the beautiful chambered nautilus that the interior became on the last steps. I thought of the cool feel of the brick, of the wear from the imprints of countless workers, keepers, and tourists. I nodded my head.

"History, Barb," I said. "History."

Carol Freas "LBI Shack"
7 1/2" x 10 1/2"
Watercolor 2000
Collection of Artist
Prints Available

Jane Law "Shack On The Causeway To Long Beach Island"
22" x 30" Watercolor 1999 Private Collection

Beverly Golembeski "Gliding Sedges"
11" x 17" Watercolor 1998 Collection of Artist Prints Available

Three Encounters With The Natural

One: The Snowy Egret

While leaving the Dutchman's restaurant on Cedar Bonnet Island, I notice a lone diner in the Manahawkin Bay. A snowy egret, white as the foam on a breaker, takes small, erratic steps on reed-like black legs. Its tiny bead of an eye peers into the water, and its body hovers just above the bay's surface, as still as a ceiling. Then, like a spring, the egret extends its S-curved neck and spears the bay's sun-glittered surface with a long, pointed bill, leaving ripples as perfect as any Olympic diver's. When it turns and faces us, I am amazed that its body seems as thin as a pair of scissors.

Nearby, swallows glide out from under the dark wooden pilings of the Long Beach Island causeway. With their fast flight and pointed wings, they skim the water by the egret for insects. A male mallard, with its glossy green head and yellow bill, sits huddled on the shore as the tide goes out, leaving behind a graveyard of clam shells, barnacled driftwood, the castoff carapaces of crabs, mussel shells, and seaweed. The rank smell prickles my nose. I wonder where the mallard's female is—nesting, maybe, or even dead. I wonder if ducks get depressed.

The snowy egret continues to forage, stirring up the bay in its search for food. I think of the French onion soup I just had in the Dutchman's—so tasty, and so easy to order. I am indeed fortunate. Overhead, cars whir along the causeway, and diners walk in and out of the Dutchman's. No one notices the egret, its bill disappearing once more among flecks of summer sun.

Two: Herring Gulls

Leaning on the railing at the four-story Ocean One Pier in Atlantic City, I witness a remarkable air show. Herring gulls glide above and below me; some hang in the air, then rise or fall on invisible elevators. One gull floats its profile in front of my face, its white body gleaming in the sunlight. Its gray wings, spread to a little over three feet, have black tips with white spots. To be an arm's length away and at eye-level with a large gull—its yellow beak obviously built for pecking—is a little disconcerting. I wonder if it is looking for food. After hanging motionless for about five seconds, it glides away.

These ubiquitous gulls are figure skaters of the air, sculpting the sky with their flight and delighting the eye. Yet they are also as wild as the sea itself. Although they live in colonies, they compete for food and space: if one drops a clam from the air to crack the hard shell, another may rush in to pick out the meat. If one is perched on a piling, another will glide in and bump it off. But when a gull finds a sudden abundance of food, such as a herring run or bait thrown away by fishermen, it will cry out to the others, and soon there are cacophonies of gull voices playing over the white noise of the waves. Below me, a woman on the beach takes a piece of her lunch and gives it to one of the gulls. Within a couple of minutes, she stands in a localized snowstorm of feathers, like some female St. Francis of Assisi.

A friend of mine who lives by the Metedeconk River awoke early one morning to several loud noises on his roof. Thinking it might be a raccoon or hailstones, he dressed and went outside to investigate. All he found were a couple of smashed crabs on the walkway; more were undoubtedly on the rooftop. It had been raining crabs, courtesy of the gulls. Another time, out on his dock, he spotted some blood and gull feathers on the boards. He wondered if a crab had gotten a claw-hold on some unfortunate gull. More deeply, he thought about the myriad life-and-death scenes played out daily that went unnoticed by everyone except those involved. He later claimed the somber thought urged him to revel in the bright summer's day, and he spent the afternoon boating with his fiancé.

Three: Horseshoe Crab

I first spotted the carapace during a nighttime walk along Barnegat Bay, as the tide was rising high and the moon hovered over the horizon. A glint of light off the wet shell caught my eye; black and domed, it had the look of a German World War II helmet. As I neared, I noticed the tapered spike protruding from one end, and realized it was a horseshoe crab—a throwback to the trilobites of Cambrian times.

I remembered how in high school I puzzled over a picture of a trilobite fossil in my outdated science textbook. I thought how much like the horseshoe crab it looked. Later, to my amazement, I discovered that the horseshoe crab goes back three hundred sixty million years—the creature thrived before the age of dinosaurs, before the continents drifted apart. Now I stood in wonder as the crab slowly dragged itself back into the bay and floated away in the moonlight, leaving behind only the straight track of its spiked tail and the scribble of claw tracks. She must have buried her eggs under the sand and the full moon, I thought. Only then did I fathom that I had just been witness to a primeval ritual, one that began eons before human beings and all their achievements and horrors. This might be as near to the eternal on Earth as I would ever come, I thought: sand, moon, stars, and the propagation of a prehistoric life form. Standing there, I stared into the moonlit bay, trying to spot the crab's shining shell, seeing only the swell of endless waves rising out of the deep, deep night.

Al Barker "Gunner's Ditch"
10" x 16" Watercolor 1987 Private Collection

The Beast

The beast escaped
leaving me only
a tale. I built
the cage even though
some say the animal
I heard never existed.
Let them slip out from
the halo of their electric
city, past far fields
before the blizzard
blows. Let them go
alone, listening
for their own breath and first
snow beginning to tick in
brittle leaves and
a beast that bellows
from another alphabet.

The Animals

These are the animals. They came to us
out of curiosity. From woods, nests, seas,
they watched us travel our roads, build our bridges.
We took them into our homes, fed and cared
for them. They watched us, love in their eyes.
They would lie with us, wait for us to return,
protect us. How they could charm us with a look.
Gradually, our poems, paintings, films came
to contain them. They gave us their newborn,
and we had names for them. Soon there were three
and four of them for each of us. We built
homes and cemeteries for them, named our cars
after them, shared our streets and walks with them.
Shelves at supermarkets stocked their food.
Their ways entered our language. The pages
of our dictionaries increased. We added
laws to the books, licensing and tagging them.
To many, they became too many.
They watched us, love in their eyes. From backyards,
black holes of doghouse and birdhouse stare.

Flamingo: At The Cape May Zoo

Your heart's
nest of
feathered flames
reposes
below the S
curved neck.
Reedy legs
grow out of
the mud that
hides your
webbed feet.
Poking
a shovel-like bill
under your
feathers
you pluck
the parasite
from your nest.
The black sequins
of those pinpoint
eyes fasten
your look.

Flamboyant
as a drag queen
you slink
down the dirt
runway by
a little girl who
shouts something
about your skinny
pink legs. In
Holiday City
plastic replicas
of you rule
the keen-green
lawns. Only
the sombreroed
man with the burro
eclipses
your flaming
numbers as
you continue
to go forth
and multiply.

Cathleen P. Engelsen "Great Blue Heron In Its Natural Habitat Along The Jersey Shore"
13 1/2" x 13 1/2" Acrylic 1993 Private Collection Prints Available

Jane Law "Salt Meadow and Marsh"
19" x 30" Watercolor 1999 Collection of the Geraldine Dodge Foundation

The Stranded

The stranded alive and the stranded dead. What is more important than life and death? Many years ago on the beach in Spring Lake, I came upon a small crowd gathered around a dead baleen whale. A couple of teenagers had climbed on top of it and begun shouting, as though playing king of the mountain. Others milled about it in awe, touching its dry, rubbery flesh, gritty with sand.

This was the first time I had ever seen a whale up close. It was also the first time I had seen baleen. I was so ignorant about whales that I asked aloud where its teeth were, and what was that thing in its mouth that looked like radiator plates. Only later did I discover that one of the Earth's largest creatures eats some of the Earth's smallest creatures (krill) by filtering the seawater with its baleen. The incident always remained with me, as I wondered about the sea world, our world, and where the two overlapped.

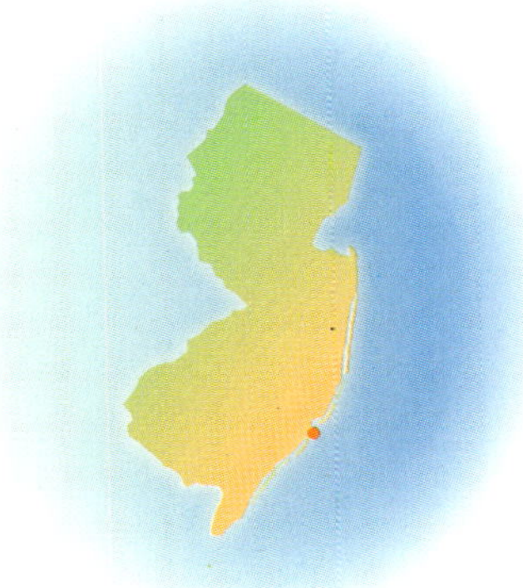

Recently, a poet friend of mine and I were walking along the shoreline of Brigantine island, just north of Atlantic City. A nature lover, she described to me how the snow geese in the fall would migrate from their breeding grounds in the Arctic and settle here by the thousands throughout the marshes, bays, and estuaries of the Edwin B. Forsythe National Wildlife Refuge. Located just north of the island, outside of Oceanville, the refuge comprises mostly tidal salt meadow and marshland, and it provides food and cover for many types of wildlife, including the snow geese. "If the water doesn't freeze, they might even stay through the winter," she said. Her voice took on a lilt as she described how their faint honking would grow louder as they approached in a loose "V" formation—a thin musical letter in the sky. When they settled, they sometimes looked like patches of snow on the marsh mud.

Continuing our walk, we spotted what looked like litter—thin, round jar sealants about six inches in diameter. Picking one off the sand, the opaque circle felt like onion-skin paper. I wondered who would litter the beach with so many of these waxy-looking lids. I then realized that they were the wilted remnants of moon jellyfish entering their last phase beneath the strong rays of the afternoon sun; soon they would vanish. A little later, we came upon a half-decayed fish that might have been a striped bass. It was a little longer than a yard and as stout as a laundry basket. Abuzz with flies, the fish gave off an unbearable stench. My friend said that the Marine Mammal Stranding Center would probably be notified to pick it up.

"What's a Marine Mammal Stranding Center, and why would they pick up a fish—and a dead fish, at that?" I asked.

My friend smiled. "They pick up dead fish so they can pinpoint on a map where they're dying, note each type, and see if there's a pattern to their deaths. Kind of like a fish detective. But that's only part of the center's job. Mainly, it tries to save stranded seals, dolphins, and other sea mammals and return them to the sea."

The stranded alive, the stranded dead. The memory of the whale in Spring Lake, with its teenagers on top, rose up from a depth of years to surface in my mind and breathe again. It seemed as if I had now discovered the one place in the state dedicated to saving these creatures and others. I decided this Marine Mammal Stranding Center deserved a closer look.

∞

I visited the center a few weeks later. Part of the Northeast Regional Stranding Network (a group of government-permit holders from Maine to Virginia that are allowed to rehabilitate marine mammals), it has three buildings: the animal rehab hospital; an administrative office; and the Sea Life Educational Center, a wooden, octagonal structure with a boardwalk and a glass cupola. The educational center includes a gift shop and a museum that offers such rare sights as a sperm whale's jawbone and a dolphin's spinal column. Standing outside its doors, I noted on display the gray skull of a humpback whale, marked with a cut from a boat propeller. An orange and black butterfly lilted on the eye socket.

Inside, I introduced myself to Bob Shoelkopf, the director and founder of the stranding center. He was in his early fifties and boyishly good looking, with smooth, sandy hair and a slim, muscular build. He was wearing a gray "Cupid the Seal" crewneck sweatshirt, one of the items they sell to raise money for the center. He quickly offered to take me on a tour.

In the museum, the walls around us and the circular ceiling above showcased a variety of marine mammals, fish, and reptiles—dolphins, seals, porpoises, sharks, sea turtles, marlin, sunfish—all swirling in frozen motion. Looking up, I felt as though I were underneath the water in a sea dream. Bob informed me they had all once been real.

"They're fiberglass castings," he said, standing by a "Please Touch" display of bleached marine mammal bones. "Our volunteer taxidermist has captured every wrinkle." Overall, the museum contained twenty-five life-size replicas of creatures that had been found in New Jersey waters. Even the stranded dead were saved here.

I asked Bob how he had become interested in this type of work. In a patient, clear voice, as though he had been asked that question many times, he told me how he once had a part-time job vacuuming the show pool at the Philadelphia Aquarium. A few nights into it, he got the strong feeling that someone was watching him. He turned around to discover

Al Barker "Barnegat Light"
13 1/4" x 18 1/4" Watercolor 1988 Private Collection Prints Available

that the four show dolphins had unhooked the gate to their enclosure and were in the tank with him. He didn't know what to do, so he kept vacuuming the pool. They were clicking, chirping, whistling, and squawking to each other as they playfully swam around and over him. Finally, the largest of them, Sinbad, grabbed the vacuum from his hands and began pushing it around the bottom. Another dove to the bottom of the pool, picked up a penny, and placed it in Bob's hand. Since that night, he had had a deep respect for their grace and beauty.

And from that respect grew the desire to help them. Bob and his wife, Sheila Dean, started the center in 1978 with the aid of a government grant and some dedicated volunteers. Their first building—a shack, really—was built from wood found on the Atlantic City beaches, and for the first eleven years the couple drew no salaries. To bring in money, she worked three jobs; he, two. Even when they became salaried, though, money continued to remain a primary focus. With state and federal funding unavailable on a yearly basis, they had to rely on donations, member fees, sales from T-shirts and sweatshirts (such as the one Bob was wearing), fundraisers, and small grants from private sources. However, hard work and dedication had helped them overcome such obstacles: since 1978, when they attended to nineteen reported strandings, the center had helped more than two thousand marine mammals and sea turtles, rehabilitating and releasing them back into the sea.

Although the staff tries not to name the animals or grow attached to them, it does sometimes happen. Such was the case with the soulful, wide-eyed animal represented on Bob's shirt, a harbor seal with a fractured jaw that the center picked up one Valentine's Day. After they fixed his jaw, the seal could have escaped a number of times, but didn't. In fact, he was so domesticated that he would fall asleep on their laps. Considering the day he was found and his loving nature, the name Cupid came naturally. Unfortunately, the accident had left Cupid's jaw slightly out of alignment (which can be seen on the sweatshirt). Since this prevented him from eating fish whole, the staff didn't release him into the sea but instead sent him to the New York Aquarium, where he lived well for seven more years.

A similar story involved Tak, a baby seal abandoned by its mother at a beach club in Sea Bright. "Humans had unintentionally frightened the mother away," Bob said. "When my wife and I got there, the baby still had the umbilical cord attached to it. Sheila raised her. Tak would play with her rubber boot and even chase butterflies. She had no inclination to leave." Tak eventually found her home in an aquarium in Indiana that had offered to take her. "We have placed seals in Ohio, Tennessee, and a number of other states," Bob added. "There's even a blind one in the Point Pleasant Aquarium that's doing quite well."

As we continued our tour, Bob introduced me to one of his field stranding technicians, Alexa Bracht. A young woman in her twenties, she was on call twenty-four hours a day and had to carry a pager at all times. She told me that winter is the busiest time for seal strandings, which only sometimes result from human interference—for example, if a seal has become tangled in rope, hit by buckshot, or cut by boat propellers. Instead, most strandings stem from natural causes such as shark bites, respiratory diseases, and other illnesses. Those seals she found that were already dead she reported to the government. "It's important to get accurate numbers of what's dying and where," she said.

Thanking Alexa, Bob and I continued on our tour. Immediately, we came upon one of the most amazing exhibits in the museum: the Ocean Sunfish, or Mola Mola. As large as a queen-size mattress, it seemed to be all head and fins. (Some people even call it a "headfish.") It had a small, bony beak with teeth, small eyes in line with its beak, and a short, scalloped tail. The fish's main line of defense was its skin: six inches thick and abrasive, it could have cut me if I tried to run my hand over it.

One of the staffers told me this one was a baby; if it stood on its tail, it would look like a ghost with two low wings. A fully grown Ocean Sunfish, however, could weigh over two thousand pounds. When I asked him if these fish swam off the Jersey Coast, he said he had seen the outline of one in the bay this summer. Usually, though, they're found in the open sea. Looking at the strange fish, I realized how little I knew about the lives of creatures that live in the ocean. I wondered what life forms might be brewing even now.

After finishing the museum tour, I briefly visited the animal rehab hospital. Located directly across from the museum and gift shop, it houses several seal enclosures, as well as an indoor pool measuring thirty feet by ten feet by four feet. Although the area was not open to the public, the pool could clearly be seen through the cyclone fence. Over the years, it had accommodated everything from dolphins to small whales. As I watched, one lone loggerhead sea turtle floated to the surface. About two feet long and weighing maybe sixty pounds, it had five big side plates and a large head. It also had a puncture wound about the size of a quarter in its carapace, the result of having been caught by the intake valve of the Oyster Creek power plant in Forked River. Staff were treating the wound and hoping to transport the turtle back to a hospital in North Carolina. Sadly, such cases were not rare; since its founding, the center had handled four hundred fifty-two loggerhead strandings. I recalled how turtle fossils date back to the age of dinosaurs, and how turtles are considered the most intelligent reptiles. Slow moving and mostly silent, they have watched other species come and go. I hoped this one would continue to do so for many years to come.

Leaving the center, a passage from Loren Eiseley's essay *The Star Thrower* came to mind. The star thrower is a man who, on a desolate shore, throws live, stranded starfish back into the sea, hoping they will live if the offshore pull is strong enough. Upon meeting him, Loren soon joins him in his appointed task. "*It was like a sowing—the sowing of life on an infinitely gigantic scale,*" he wrote, then later added, "*Somewhere… there is a hurler of stars, and he walks, because he chooses, always in desolation, but not in defeat.*" After meeting some of the people at the center, I felt I had found that "somewhere." And I was glad of it.

Greg Rogers
"Cormorant At Sunset On Beaver Dam Creek"
15" x 22" Watercolor 1990
Collection of Artist

Robert A. Loder Jr. "The Flanders Of Ocean City"
24" x 36" Acrylic 1994 Private Collection Prints Available

Gamboling In A.C.

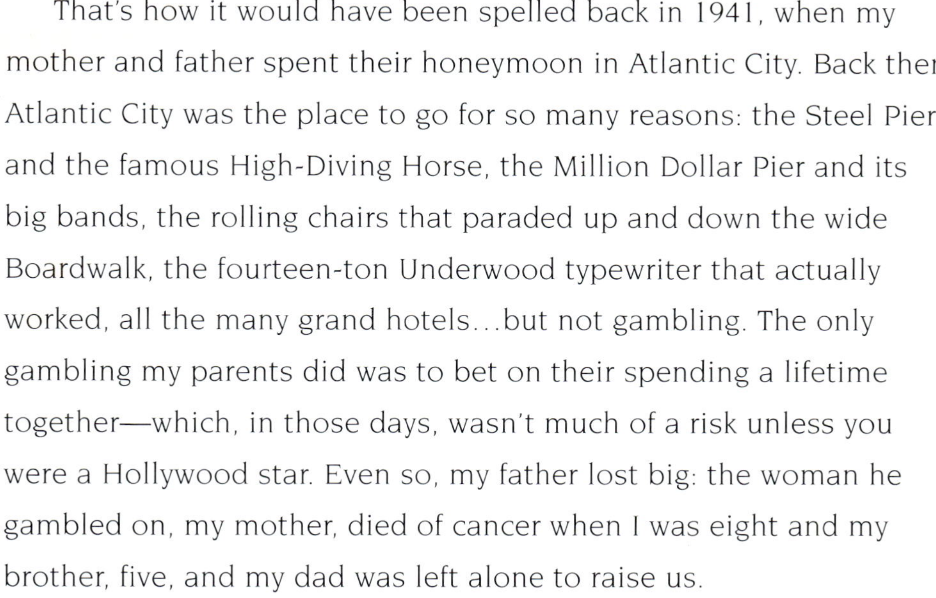

That's how it would have been spelled back in 1941, when my mother and father spent their honeymoon in Atlantic City. Back then, Atlantic City was the place to go for so many reasons: the Steel Pier and the famous High-Diving Horse, the Million Dollar Pier and its big bands, the rolling chairs that paraded up and down the wide Boardwalk, the fourteen-ton Underwood typewriter that actually worked, all the many grand hotels…but not gambling. The only gambling my parents did was to bet on their spending a lifetime together—which, in those days, wasn't much of a risk unless you were a Hollywood star. Even so, my father lost big: the woman he gambled on, my mother, died of cancer when I was eight and my brother, five, and my dad was left alone to raise us.

Today, in what has become a far different Atlantic City, I have come to the Boardwalk with my own wife, Barb, to make a quite different wager—one that involves slot machines, roulette wheels, or any of the other games of chance that have become a part of this city's identity. Although Barb is a veteran of the casinos—she and her mother come twice a year to gamble a few rolls of quarters—this will be my first time, and the prospect has me feeling surprisingly buoyant, as well as a little nervous. Stepping onto the Boardwalk, I can't help but think back to my parents and their time here, and to all the bad luck that followed—Pearl Harbor, America's entrance into World War II, death. I try to rid myself of the bad thoughts, and instead concentrate on how this is the city where my parents enjoyed a magical week, the city where they laughed and danced and rode in rolling chairs, the city where I believed I was conceived. I give Barb's hand a quick squeeze as we head up the Boardwalk, the wooden slats blurring beneath our feet.

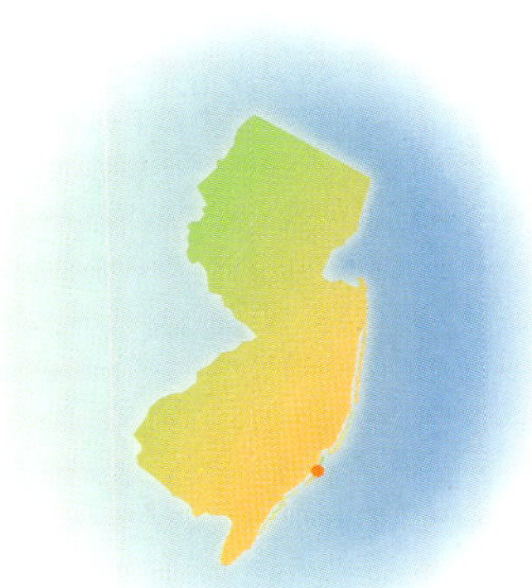

Barb turns to me. "What's that for?" she asks.

"Luck," I say, and squeeze again.

Stephen Harrington "Absecon Light, N.J. 1882"
20" x 16" Ink, Watercolor, Color Pencil 1998 Collection of Artist Prints Available

Stephen Harrington "Absecon Light, N.J. 1927"
20" x 16" Ink, Watercolor, Color Pencil 1998 Collection of Artist Prints Available

Walking with Barb, her hand in mine, I begin to relax. I look out toward the Atlantic; the tang of the sea air hits me full in the face, and I am soothed by the sound of the waves—*shooorasheee*—breaking along the beach. As we near the casino, though, I begin hearing a low, eerie sound, like the hum of some ominous machine that keeps the place running. Thinking I am imagining it, I ask Barb if she hears it too.

"What sound?" she asks.

"That humming," I say with a bit of anxiety; *was* I hearing things?

"Oh, that. That's coming from the casino."

And as soon as we walk through the glass-plate front doors, I discover immediately what she means: hundreds of slot and video poker machines are giving off their musical, triumphant sounds, *thwacks* and *whirs* and *ding-ding-dings*, and change going *ka-chink ka-chink ka-chink*. In a way, it *is* the sound of the machinery that keeps the place running. I shake my head; it's a far cry from the sound of breaking waves.

Taking a small, plastic bucket from a stack between two slot machines, I head toward the cashier to exchange a twenty dollar bill for two rolls of quarters. As I wait, I notice that I am surrounded by older people—all of whom look to be well past retirement age—and am surprised not only by the number, but also by the odds that they have overcome to get here. Some arrive with walkers and three-pronged canes, others maneuver wheelchairs or oxygen tanks through the crowd. One woman behind me clutches an empty bucket in her right hand, and in her left she grips the handle of an oxygen tank; a small rubber hose runs from the tank to her nostrils. At a quick glance, this crowd could be a throng of pilgrims at Lourdes, waiting for a miracle cure. The urge to gamble cuts through all ages, it seems—as well as all colors, ethnicities, and income brackets.

The man behind the exchange cage breaks my twenty and hands me two packets of rolled quarters. I like the heft of them in my palm. Giving Barb one, I take the other, tear it open, and let the coins clunk into the bucket. After agreeing to stop when the quarters are gone, Barb gives me a quick kiss on the cheek and sets off to find her favorite slot machine.

I begin to look for a slot that's open, taking note of the people I pass in the aisles. One white-haired woman with a leathery tan stares at her machine as though she's in a deep trance; she pulls the lever, quarter after quarter, even after the machine dings her with wins. K*er-chunk* goes the lever, again and again. Another woman passes me, saying, "I just know there's an ATM machine around here somewhere." Everyone seems mesmerized, a feeling that's only accentuated by the many lights and mirrors that seem to pour into one another. Round light bulbs—red, yellow, green, and blue—appear everywhere, swagged from hook to hook on the ceiling. By a casino restaurant, twinkle-lights wrap around the branches of an indoor tree. Above me, neon lights rise on ascending wires and reach the high ceiling, creating a circus "Big Top" of lights. It's all very bewitching.

Meanwhile, every slot I pass beckons: Jolly/Roger, Great White, Bee Zerk, Triple Diamonds, Wheel of Fortune, Jokers Wild, each with its own set of rules for a win. I settle down before a Triple Diamonds machine. A woman two machines down is smiling and looking around the casino excitedly, as her machine erupts with flashing lights and bells. When I look at her, she apparently feels obligated to tell me that she's waiting for the floor person to confirm her win—one thousand dollars. (When a big win happens, it's casino policy to confirm it on the floor and pay in large bills.) "I have enough to eat dinner out now," she smiles. I wonder what one thousand dollars in quarters weighs. A floor person, wearing a red uniform

Dawn Hotaling "Carousel"
19" x 24 1/2" Watercolor 2000 Collection of Artist Prints Available

Dawn Hotaling "Dealer's Break"
25" x 36" Watercolor 2000
Collection of Artist Prints Available

jacket, arrives with the payment. People nearby stop, look, and listen with dreamy smiles at this person's money train coming in.

Hoping for similar luck, I place a quarter in the slot and pull down the black stick with its red bulbous-clown-nose handle. The three tumblers spin and stop one by one: cherries, diamonds, a seven. No win. I play again with another quarter. Nothing. Another quarter. Press, spin. Zilch. Thinking this will be one quick trip to Atlantic City, I play again—and hit. With a succession of five quick dings, the numeral five lights up in the credit box. An almost electric excitement begins coursing through me as I press the "Three Max" button and spin. Nothing. Play one. Two diamonds spin into place—a hit. The machine begins to *ding*—and *ding*, and *ding*, and each time it does my stomach does a little flip. It stops at twenty, and I press the "Cash In" button. Twenty quick *ka-chinks* as twenty quarters cover a part of the metal tray below. I scoop them up and place them in my container, eager for more. Already I am like one of Pavlov's conditioned dogs, salivating for the *dings* and *ka-chinks* I can get by placing more quarters in the slot. I can't help it. I stuff five more coins into the machine, pull down the handle.

I lose a host of quarters, hitting some fives and tens along the way, before hitting another twenty. As I did before, I immediately begin feeding them back into the machine. The tumblers spin, and spin, and spin again, but now the machine refuses to cooperate. That doesn't stop me, though; almost robotically, I keep feeding quarters into the slot, as if I were now part of the machinery that keeps this place running. My arm becomes an extension of the machine. I don't think, don't wonder; I just play. And play. By the time Barb shows up with an empty bucket, I am down to my last few quarters. She begs a few off of me, plays them in the next slot, and loses.

Barb's appearance breaks the spell, and I stop dropping quarters into the machine. Before coming down here, I did a little research and discovered that an estimated sixteen million Americans have experienced gambling problems, according to the National Research Council. Looking at the few lonely quarters left in my bucket, I begin to understand why. "I should've left when I hit that last twenty," I grumble. "Let me just finish these and we'll leave." I play two of my remaining quarters and spin. The tumblers stop at three diamonds.

The machine won't stop dinging. *Ding, ding, ding, ding*...all my sad thoughts of losses and gambling problems evaporate, and the whole world centers around this wonderful machine and its musical march, its counter ticking off my new-found wealth. *Ding, ding, ding, ding*...I try counting them off, then delightedly give up. *Ding, ding, ding, ding*...on and on it goes. I fall in love with that sound, cannot bear to think it will end. For what seems like hours, it doesn't. When the machine finally turns silent, the marker has stopped at two hundred. 2-0-0. I look at Barb, who is gripping my arm.

"Cash in, Frank," she says. "Don't throw it all away. Take it now."

I press "Cash In" and am greeted with a new sound: *ka-chink, ka-chink, ka-chink*...I try to decide which sound I like better, then just watch as the quarters splash into the metal tray. Finally, the last coin drops. I scoop through the pile with one hand and feel like Disney's Scrooge McDuck, who would sit on his vaulted mountain of coins and run his gloved hands through them. Slowly, Barb and I begin transferring them to my bucket, which I now notice is colored green—the color of money.

I take the dictionary-heavy bucket up to the caged cashier. He places three quarters on the side and puts the rest on the change counter. Numbers flash on the small screen as quickly as the years passed in the old time-travel movies. They stop at fifty-one dollars and twenty-five cents. The cashier puts in the other three quarters and hands me two twenties, a ten, and two singles.

When we emerge from the casino, it is twilight. The casino's hot neon burns under the darkening sky, as if it is absorbing all the light. Barb and I move a few yards down the Boardwalk and sit on one of the oceanside benches, under a sprinkle of stars.

"Congratulations, Mr. Finale," Barb says. "You've beaten the casinos. You're a winner."

I shake my head. The earlier euphoria has vanished, as if the sound of the waves had washed me clean. "I just as easily could have walked away broke—in fact, I almost did," I say. "If we had lost a few quarters more, we would never have gotten the chance to win big."

Winning big, losing big. The thought of my father returns: we all make many gambles in this lifetime, have so many chances to lose or win. I stare out at the Atlantic, at the whitecaps forming and breaking on the beach. Did he and my mother sit just like this, back in 1941, under the same stars whose light came from so many centuries past? I try to imagine the joy and excitement of the two newlyweds, as well as their anticipation of the night to come. I think back to, as a child, paging through my parents' photo albums of Atlantic City postcards, and the gleam that came to their eyes when I asked about them. I look over at Barb, her red hair blowing in the salt wind, her green eyes filled with bright promise and mystery as they stare out at the ocean, and I suddenly know how my father must have felt sitting next to my mother. And that feeling is worth any gamble.

Putting my hand into my left pocket, I pull out a $20 bill. "Want to take a chance with me?" I whisper into Barb's ear. I stand up and motion to one of the rolling chair drivers, who immediately stops. Helping her into the hooded seat, I give Barb's hand a squeeze. "For luck," I say.

Barb smiles. "You don't need it. You've got a sure thing," she says, her green eyes filled with mischief. And then we head down the Boardwalk, under the moon and stars, listening to the ocean speak, much as my mother and father must have done so many years before. I don't know what tomorrow will bring, but that's all right. Tonight, I'm a winner.

Stephen Harrington "Hereford Inlet Light, N.J. 1918"
12" x 16" Ink, Watercolor, Color Pencil 1996
Collection of Artist Prints Available

Nicholas P. Santoleri "A View Of Columbia Avenue"
18" x 39 1/2" Watercolor 1996 Private Collection Prints Available

Patricia Rainey "The Queen Victoria"
20" x 16" Watercolor 1996
Collection of Artist Prints Available

Weekend In Cape May

Angel of the Sea, the Wedding Cake House, Sea Holly Inn, the Abbey, the Gingerbread House, the Pink House...Barb and I passed each one as we drove toward the Queen Victoria, our favorite of Cape May's many inns. Actually, we weren't driving directly *toward* the Queen Victoria; rather, we were casually cruising around the narrow streets of Cape May, trying to take in the unusual and intricate configurations of the many Victorian houses with their porches, columns, towers, peaks, cupolas, and gingerbread trim.

"Look at that one!" Barb said, pointing to a tower with arched windows that rose above the sidewalk trees. "It could be right out of a Gothic novel!"

"Maybe it's haunted," I said, slowing down and gazing up at the iron railing that rimmed the top of the five-stories-high tower. For that moment, I half-expected to see a weatherbeaten sea captain gazing out toward where his four-masted bark once sailed the high seas.

As we passed the Pink House, Barb pointed excitedly. "Oooh, it looks almost good enough to eat!"

"I think you're just hungry, Barb," I said. Still, looking at the inn's pink-confection clapboard and white gingerbread trim, I couldn't help but feel my own sweet tooth begin to stir.

On we drove, feeling like two kids gazing through a kaleidoscope—with each street corner we turned, we found another astonishing combination of colors and forms. Finally, while driving down Ocean Street, we spotted the Queen Victoria, perched on its corner one block in from the ocean. "It feels good to see the familiar façade again," I said, and Barb nodded. Every April for the past several years, Barb and I had come here for a short "getaway" vacation, and it had become a tradition we both happily anticipated. Built by a Delaware River pilot in 1881 and later restored, the inn has a mansard roof, sloped turrets, gables, and a red-brick chimney—all the requisite Victorian charms. The bottom two floors, painted in an eye-refreshing mint green, have high arched windows, while the third floor is done in a pinkish-red, as if it had taken on the color of the many sunsets it had witnessed. While the Queen Victoria is just one of more than six hundred Victorian structures in Cape May's Primary Historic District, for us it had become a favorite spot to experience the ambiance that led to the local catch phrase, "Our Future Is In Our Past."

Pulling into the driveway, we spotted Joan Wells, the innkeeper. A passionate gardener, she was kneeling and religiously tending the alyssum and heather that grew along the small iron fence bordering the property. At the sound of our tires she looked up, and her smile bloomed.

"Frank, Barbara, how wonderful to see you again!" Wiping her hands, she quickly walked over to where we were retrieving our overnight bags from the trunk, then led us toward the front porch. Shaded by a green-and-white striped awning, the porch had enough rocking chairs to make a confident cat nervous. Looking at them, I remembered the many evenings when Barb and I had sat there, as the last of the sunlight touched the alyssum and the first stars appeared overhead. Walking up the front steps, I couldn't help but feel as if I had arrived home.

After checking in, Barb and I went to the inn's next-door annex, Prince Albert Hall, and climbed the stairs to our second-floor room. This was where we usually stayed, and, upon entering, we found nothing much had changed. It still had the same sitting area with a small TV, a mini-refrigerator, a settee, and a marble-top coffee table with magazines such as *Smithsonian*, *Life*, and *Travel*. It also had the same queen-size, canopied, wrought-iron bed with the thick mattress and fluffy pillows that, as always, immediately lured us in. We both slipped off our shoes, plumped down on the bed, and sighed our comfort. Turning toward each other, we lightly kissed. "Two days and nights all to ourselves," Barb said, smiling. "Free at last!" I exclaimed, and raised my arms as if in triumph.

One of the many reasons Barb, who has arthritis, likes to return here is for the whirlpool tub and special herbal bath grains. The first thing she always does upon arriving is to soak in the tub for twenty minutes or so; it relaxes her aches, bubbles away her stress, and, with sweet scents, refreshes her disposition. That afternoon was no different. Ritualistically, she set up the things she needed—towel, shampoo, conditioner, a special body lotion, loofah, and book to read. After preparing the bathwater, she slipped in, leaving only her head showing in the ghostly vapors above the water, and began humming a mysterious tune. It was her river of Lethe, where she could forget the bills, her pain, the many things that might have gone wrong over the weeks and months. I knew that when she emerged from the foam of bubbles like Aphrodite, it would be as if she were reborn. "I'm ready to take on the world," she always said, and she looked it.

While Barb hummed and soaked, I sprawled on the bed and gazed out the window into the leaves of a nearby tree. Somehow, it enraptured and transported me back to childhood, when I would climb the maple tree in our front yard, draw strength from its trunk, feel connected to the earth and closer to the sky. It released my imagination, and I dreamed about faraway places. Each leaf was a different land: Istanbul, Prague, Lisbon, Athens, Singapore...I closed my eyes, imagined going down a cobblestoned street of cafes and small shops selling incense, spirits, candies...

"Are you going to use the whirlpool?" Barb interrupted my reveries, her shining hair slowly dripping onto the carpet. I looked at the clock; a half hour had passed, even though it had felt like only five minutes. "No, I'll just shower; it's

Nicholas P. Santoleri "After Labor Day"
17 3/4" x 40" Watercolor 1995 Private Collection

Nicholas P. Santoleri "Angel Of The Sea"
22 1/2" x 34 1/2" Watercolor 1997
Private Collection Prints Available

quicker," I said, and immediately wondered who conditioned me so well to save time. What would I do with the fifteen minutes I saved? Too bad I couldn't accumulate the time and donate it to someone who might need it. It especially seemed out of place here; Cape May was not a place to track time, but to meander, to get lost, and to find one's self again.

After I showered and dressed, we decided to go for a walk. Gaslight lampposts adorned the thin-as-six-o'clock walks as we ambled up one street and down another, gazing at the many pastel-colored houses. White-picket or wrought-iron fences bordered gardens of tulips, daffodils, pansies, hyacinth, and lilac. One street had a sign tacked onto an elm that swelled the sidewalk and tilted the curbing. "Caution, trees lean out into the street," it read. We were delighted to find nature being given the right of way in a town that seemed to have appeared out of time, like Brigadoon.

Barb let out of sigh of contentment. "Sometimes I wish we could just move here, find a little Victorian cottage and spend the rest of our days able to walk these streets anytime we wanted."

"Ah, but then it wouldn't be special," I said.

"Either that, or every day would be," she countered. "I just want things to go at a quieter pace. Think about it: you teach all day, you come home bone-tired, you nap, you eat dinner, then you go back to your writing until you can barely make it to the bed and drop off to sleep. And I feel I'm constantly running—to the supermarket, to my mother's, to any of the million places I have to be on a given day. Tell me, when was the last time we actually fell asleep in each other's arms?"

I stopped short. "What does that have to do with anything?" I said. "You think there's something wrong?" I could hear the annoyance in my voice—not because the question had been asked, but because I couldn't provide an answer.

Barb smiled and took my hand. "Not at all. I'm just saying that life—normal, daily life—seems to sneak up on us, and sometimes it would be nice to slow down. That's all." She leaned over and kissed my cheek, and whatever tension I had felt immediately evaporated—as if I, too, had entered my own river of Lethe. Or maybe it was just because the day was too perfect to spoil. I looked at Barb, her red curls bouncing in the sun, her freckled hand circling mine; her green eyes took in everything, from the highest spire to the smallest petal, and the entire street seemed to center around her intensity and light. Looking at her, I wondered why in the world I would ever *not* have her in my arms every chance I could.

We made it back to the Queen Victoria in time for high tea, which is usually served at 4:00 P.M. at a long, heavy, wooden table in the dining room. Before returning to our room, we stopped in the sitting room to look over the menus from area restaurants; all of the walking had made us long for an early dinner. After going back and forth between seafood or Italian, formal or relaxed, we finally decided on a place called Tricia's, which had a romantic waterfront location, a nice range of entrees, and a BYOB policy that would ensure we could bring our favorite chardonnay. It seemed a little pricey, but we wanted something special. After all, it wasn't every day we were able to step back into the Victorian era.

Our choice couldn't have been better. After stopping to pick up the chardonnay, we walked the few blocks up Beach Avenue to the boardwalk. The restaurant extended on a pier over the beach, and one wall of windows looked out toward where the whitecaps broke along the coastline, creating scalloped outlines along the sand. We were seated by a window, and the waiter came immediately to light the candle on our table and take our order. We both chose the smoked salmon appetizer, then Barb ordered her usual, veal marsala,

Carole Clarke "John F. Craig House"
26" x 34" Watercolor 1999 Prints Available

while I asked for the prime rib, rare. The waiter went off and quickly returned with an ice bucket and two glasses for the chardonnay.

The meal was one of the most delicious we've ever had: the salmon and veal were so tender you barely needed a knife, and the prime rib seemed to be two inches thick. Between courses, the waiter brought us small dishes of lemon sorbet to cleanse our palates, and at the end of the meal he set two finger bowls before us. Sitting in the candlelight, as the fire of the setting sun streaked across the western sky, I raised my glass. "Here's to the good life," I said.

We toasted, and the sound of the crystal struck a perfect note.

We finally emerged from the restaurant to a night sky of stars and a sickle moon, with the surf sighing in the background and the turrets and cupolas glowing in the ghostly moonlight. Or maybe they just seemed to glow as we walked toward the inn, Barb's hand once again in mine, and all seeming right with the world. Back in our suite that mood continued: we found our bed turned down, the room tidied up, and a piece of dark chocolate—Barb's favorite—wrapped in gold-colored foil on the pillow. This was one of the things I enjoyed most about the Queen Victoria: good service, with chocolate thrown in. I always felt as though elves had come in when we weren't around, cleaned up the place, and left a little gift.

Barb and I quickly undressed and slipped between the sheets. She leaned over and kissed me. "It was a beautiful day," she said.

"It doesn't get any better."

"Here, I have a present for you." She took her chocolate, unwrapped the foil, and held it up as if it were an actual gold coin. "From me to you, Mr. Finale."

"But you love this chocolate—it's your favorite!" I protested.

"No," she said. "*You're* my favorite. And every day, by the way, is special with you." She kissed my lips. "Some are just more special than others."

She reached over and turned out the light. The rest of the night went just as perfectly as the day, and when we finally did fall asleep, we were holding each other as if we would never let go.

The Artist

She cannot see us as we look on
from the tinted window of the Cape May
Ferry. She sits in a yellow dress
on the rocks far below
and records on a sketch pad what we do not
see. A white cat brushes her ankles
and springs up onto a higher rock to be
petted. The lady in yellow strokes its white
fur and continues sketching as she watches
the boat leave port. She sees the whole
boat as part of the scene, yet never
the detail of us behind the tinted glass,
watching. Many times I see the details
but rarely the whole. This time, for an instant,
I see both, as the ferry makes its daily
departure for Cape May. I begin to write.

Stephen Harrington "Cape May Light, N.J. 1897"
20" x 16" Ink, Watercolor, Color Pencil 1996 Collection of Artist Prints Available

Donna Ayers was born and raised in Spring Lake, New Jersey. With artistic talent evident from early childhood, she dedicated herself to developing her skills. After graduating at the top of her class from the Rhode Island School Of Design, she advanced with further training in New York and Paris. Since 1985, Donna has worked full time as a professional artist. In 1991, she made the decision to specialize in portraits, declining other work. Donna continues to live and work in Monmouth County, New Jersey.

Al Barker was born in New Jersey and raised in the New York City / metropolitan area, where he learned to appreciate the outdoors by hunting and fishing. These activities led him to pursue academic studies in environmental science: he earned B. A. and M. A. degrees in forestry and later received a national fellowship for doctorate work. Al became a forestry educator, worked in private industry, and eventually taught his trade on the post-secondary level. Presently a full-time artist, Al specializes in smaller-sized paintings, completing works in both oil and watercolor as well as rendering many small editions of etchings. He has won over fifty major awards in premier art competitions and principal exhibitions, including those of the Grand National American Artists Professional League and The Salmagundi Club in New York. Al's work can be seen in almost every national miniature exhibition in the continental United States.

Alan S. Brown exhibits his work extensively in the New York / metropolitan area. His style varies greatly from photo-realistic to expressionistic, always with the figure as his central focus. "My paintings are not made in a narrative form, though they are charged images. I come upon them by combining visual elements that can be connected by the viewer." Alan has his work in many prestigious collections. These include the offices of The Supreme Court Of New Jersey; Jersey Shore Medical Center in Neptune, New Jersey; Dickinson University in Carlisle, Pennsylvania; Union County Courthouse in New Brunswick, New Jersey; and the personal collection of the former Governor of New Jersey, Jim Florio. He received a B. S. in fine art from Skidmore College in Saratoga Springs, New York, and an M. F. A. from Pratt Institute in Brooklyn, New York.

Carole Clarke, a watercolorist, is best known for her detailed paintings of porches. She has found a wealth of inspiration in Cape May's historic district. Her quest is to capture the light and shadow of a particular time of day along with the spirit and essence of a particular time in history. An award-winning artist, she is a descendant of artist Margery Ryerson (1886-1989), who together with Robert Henri compiled the book *The Art Spirit*. Carole's collection is exhibited annually at the historic Chalfonte in Cape May, New Jersey. She is represented at the Washington Street Gallery in Cape May and Deck The Walls. Carole currently resides in northern New Jersey.

Barbara J. Cocker was born in Massachusetts and studied at Becker Junior College and Mount St. Mary College. A resident of Rumson, New Jersey, Barbara specializes in painting marine subjects exclusively. The sea and its splendid moving tapestry of color, light, and form have captivated her for thirty years. Barbara is known throughout the United States and is recognized in Europe as well. Her work is included in many prestigious private and corporate collections. She has exhibited at the National Academy and the National Arts Club in New York. Her work is included in the Warner Brothers Collection in Burbank, California, The Sun Trust Banks of Florida, and PNC Banks. She is a member of the Pen And Brush Club of New York, as well as many other notable associations. She is listed in *Who's Who Of American Art*, *Who's Who Of American Women*, and was recently elected to the Coast Guard Art Program in New York.

Carla Coutts-Miners graduated from Moore College Of Art in Philadelphia, where she studied illustration. She went on to a career in advertising (concentrating on clientele in the tourism industry), using her illustration and design talents as an art director in San Francisco, California, and Bucks County, Pennsylvania. Peddler's Village in Lahaska, Pennsylvania, the Bucks County Historic Tourist Commission, and the Philadelphia Convention And Visitors Bureau all have used her fanciful art. She worked as a graphic designer for *Philadelphia Magazine* from 1990 to 1997. Her work can be found in the printed materials for Tuckerton Seaport in New Jersey and can be seen in galleries in New Jersey, Pennsylvania, and on ArtPrints.com. Original works are handled exclusively by Newman Galleries in Philadelphia. Coutts-Miners and her husband live in southern Ocean County at the Jersey Shore.

Symon Cowles was born in New York City, where he earned a graduate degree in liberal arts. His studies took him to the Art Students League in New York, The Montclair Museum of Art in New Jersey, and The Yard School of Art in Montclair, and he has traveled extensively through the art centers of Europe. He is a resident-artist member of The Salmagundi Club in New York, and is active in the Manasquan River Group Of Artists in New Jersey. Symon's landscapes, seascapes, and classical still life paintings are executed in oils, acrylics, and pastels in a contemporary realist style. He currently exhibits his paintings in New Jersey at Thistledown Gallery in Spring Lake, Anchor & Palette Gallery in Bay Head, The Jacklyn Kling Gallery in Montclair, as well as at the gallery at The Salmagundi Club in New York. Symon resides in Sea Girt, New Jersey, and New York City.

Kate Leigh Cutler is a native of beachfront Mantoloking, New Jersey. Her watercolors express her lifelong fascination with the natural landscape. She passionately uses light and location to imbue her work with emotion and color. Inspired through observation, one experiences her art with all their senses. An honors graduate of Philadelphia's Moore College Of Art And Design, she has received many creativity awards. As a result of her interior architectural training and knowledge of construction details, her custom house portraits are created with realism, depth, and charm. She has also been corporately commissioned by Lenox, Inc., Tiffany & Co. and Continental Airlines. Kate's art can be found in coastal galleries in Bay Head, New Jersey, the San Juan Islands, Washington, and Bermuda.

Cathleen P. Engelsen is an Ocean County native with a deep appreciation of New Jersey's rich, historical background and its breath taking coastal scenery. She studied art at Samuel Fleischer Art Memorial in Philadelphia, Philadelphia College Of Art, and Stockton State College in New Jersey. She paints in all medias—watercolor, acrylic, and oil. She is particularly noted in New Jersey for her highly researched historical paintings. She was commissioned by McDonald's restaurant to complete a series of historical paintings in Toms River, Manahawkin, Lakehurst, Burlington, Howell, and Ocean Township. In addition, her historical paintings of Newark, Trenton, Burlington, and Perth Amboy are in the executive and public offices of Public Service Electric and Gas. A particular favorite of Revolutionary War buffs is Cathleen's painting of Cannon Green at Princeton University.

Dede Esenlohr, a lifelong New Jersey resident, is a self-proclaimed naturalist and conservationist. She is committed to making her statements on behalf of the environment and historic places through art. Her palette-knife, acrylic technique incorporates muted tones and the subtlety of nature in a semi-impressionistic style. Dede's work reflects many years of decisive and energetic attitude as she promotes the well-being of wildlife by celebrating its habitats. Her work is influenced by the seasons, weather, and history around her, with a particular affinity toward water and its many reflections. Much of her time has been devoted to arts development. Dede's work hangs in private collections and public places worldwide.

Dennis Foy is an artist, chef, and restaurateur. Born in 1951, he attended classes at the New School in New York. He also studied with the great western landscape painters, Steve Adams and Russell Chatham, as well as with the neo-classical surrealist Mark Spencer. He is represented by Pacifico Fine Arts in New York, New York, Thistledown Gallery in Spring Lake, New Jersey, and Anchor & Palette Gallery in Bay Head, New Jersey.

Carol Freas grew up on Long Beach Island, New Jersey. Her work explores the illusive, unpredictable qualities of transparent watercolor using integrity to preserve unique images of the past. Graduating with a B. A. in art education from Kutztown State College in Pennsylvania, she has taught in New York, Florida, and Virginia, and is presently with the Long Beach Island Art Foundation and Pine Shores Art Association. Other studies with national painters led to numerous awards and purchases for private and corporate collections and acceptance as a signature artist with the Philadelphia Watercolor Society. She is available for commission and freelance work in graphic design as well as portraits in watercolor. She is affiliated with Watermark Gallery in Tuckerton, New Jersey, and Seamans Landing in Barnegat Light, New Jersey

Lloyd Garrison is a mostly self-taught artist and started his career in Rahway, New Jersey, in 1966. His style is realistic, but the subject matter is unlimited: Revolutionary War, Civil War, landscapes, still lifes, portraits, surrealism, aviation, nautical, westerns, wildlife, and florals are a few of his specialties. He has painted miniature oils, two series of Christmas plates for the Bradford Exchange, and drew comic books for two years with Gold Key Comics. Some advertisements include the cover for "Old Spice" cologne, the logo for "Sleep Doctor," and a cover for "Finley" tea. He painted murals in New Jersey for Prudential Insurance in Newark, Rahway Savings Institution, and the restaurants Barbary Coast, Brass Bucket, and Al Dente in Piscataway. His paintings can be found in the homes of known playwrights, actors, and sports figures. His wife, Lori, operates their gallery, Lloyd's Gallery, in Red Bank, New Jersey.

Beverly Golembeski is a graduate of Montclair University in New Jersey. Over the past twenty years, she has studied with watercolor professionals including C. Reid, F. Webb, S. Szabo, and N. Engle. She is a member of the New Jersey American Artists Professional League, the Garden State Watercolor Society, and the Philadelphia and Pennsylvania Watercolor Societies. She served on the board of the New Jersey Watercolor Society and was president of the Ocean County Artists' Guild for two years. Beverly is also an official artist for the United States Coast Guard and a fellow of the National American Artists' Professional League. Beverly teaches, conducts workshops, and demonstrates throughout New York, New Jersey, Maine, and Florida. Her paintings are in private and corporate collections and are available in New Jersey through the Annex Gallery in Surf City and Cricketts in Seaside Park.

Tine Kirkland Graham was inspired by childhood summers spent in Bay Head, New Jersey. She depicts her unforgettable memories of the shore in her paintings. Acrylics allow her the freedom to express her vision of the shore in unique seascapes and beach scenes, which dance and sway with rhythmic color and emotion in celebration of life as a joyous occasion. Her brilliant colors, brushed with strength and life, evoke the innocence and joys we have all experienced on vacation. To look at her work is to remind oneself that life can and should be fun. In addition to her painting, Tine's artistry encompasses graphic design and murals. Her work can be found in New Jersey at Anchor & Palette Gallery in Bay Head and at her studio and home in Morristown.

Stephen Harrington established his business, Coastal Guardians, in 1994 for the sole purpose of presenting our nation's lighthouses from a historical perspective. Each light is visited, photographed, and researched for historical accuracy. Working in cooperation with the light's historian/director, a time period reflecting the lighthouse's peak operation is selected, and the details are refined to present a rendition that is as historically accurate as possible. Each print is accompanied by a one- or two-page history. Stephen resides in Virginia Beach, Virginia.

Ann Hayes has been painting the beaches and beach-goers of the Jersey Shore since childhood. Her family bought and sold summer homes at the shore, and the excitement of exploring large, rambling architecture and discovering intimate ocean views in each new home fueled her creativity. Her training in the art of traditional, transparent watercolor began at the studio of Earl Tyler in Bay Head, New Jersey. She is best known for her commissioned watercolors and oil paintings of porch scenes, beach scenes, and the sun-drenched innocence of children at play. Ann holds a B. A. in fine art from Douglas College followed by studies at Pratt Institute in New York City. She is represented in New Jersey by Anchor & Palette Gallery in Bay Head, Thistledown Gallery in Spring Lake, and PMP Inc. in Montclair. Her studio is in Toms River.

Linda Hejduk was born in scenic New England in the small town of Stoughton, Massachusetts. After graduating in 1965 with a B. F. A. from Massachusetts College Of Art in Boston, she went on to study in Massachusetts pastel portraiture with the Robert Arthur Studio in Brockton, and watercolors with Marshall W. Joyce in Kingston. Linda then began a long, successful career in advertising graphics, storyboard illustration, and design in New York. Her talent is best reflected in acrylics and watercolors. Her works have appeared at various venues in New England, New York, and New Jersey. A member of the Ossining Arts Council in New York and the Manasquan River Group Of Artists in New Jersey, Linda divides her time between homes in Scarborough, New York, and Mantoloking, New Jersey.

Dawn Hotaling is a watercolorist whose roots have grown strong in the shores of New Jersey. Her work has grown from its origins in architectural paintings to now include the figure caught unaware in a moment of work or play. Dawn exhibits nationally—her original paintings and thousands of her prints can be found from Alaska to Australia. Her recent focus is helping emerging artists deal with promotional and marketing challenges. Visit her website at www.dawnhotaling.netmegs.com.

Beth Alyse Kantor was born in Aberdeen, New Jersey and studied art history at Princeton University. After graduating in 1998, her work has been displayed in four solo shows and in as many group exhibitions throughout the tri-state area and California. Beth has received numerous awards, including being named a finalist in the *American Artist Magazine's* Realism Today competition. She was also among fifteen artists, from across the country, selected to participate in a painting seminar held at the Forbes Ranch in Colorado, culminating in a spring exhibition at the Forbes Gallery in New York and an accompanying feature article in *Watercolor Magazine*. Beth is currently represented in New Jersey by Anchor & Palette Gallery in Bay Head, Dorothy Carrol Art Gallery in Stone Harbor, Spring Lake Gallery in Spring Lake, as well as Long View Gallery in Sperryville, Virginia.

Edward J. Kojola is known for his illustrative paintings and drawings. He is a graduate of Pratt Institute. He enjoys painting images of a mechanical nature and researches extensively before starting a painting to ensure all details are accurate. He says, "Doing color studies make the final painting a snap." Ed often includes personal numerical facts, including his birth date, in the design. His watercolors have been exhibited at juried shows throughout New Jersey, winning many awards. His painting "*Holmdel* U. S. A.," for which he received a Senate resolution, was on loan to the New Jersey State Senate in Trenton. Private collectors have commissioned Ed's work. His Holmdel studio is filled with many works in progress.

Paula Kolojeski has been painting the New Jersey Shore in pastels for over twenty years. Working on location, she enjoys capturing the effects of light on sand and sea. Her work has won awards in many juried shows and is found in collections throughout the United States as well as Canada, Europe, Saudi Arabia, and Japan. She is represented by Main Street Gallery in Manasquan, New Jersey, where originals and limited edition reproductions of her work are available. Her work is featured on their website: www.mainstreetgallery.com. Paula resides in Princeton, New Jersey.

Dick LaBonté began to paint professionally in his fifties after he took early retirement from *Business Week* magazine in New York. His neo-primitive acrylic scenes of bygone days at the New Jersey Shore caught on quickly. These and other prints are sold along the eastern seaboard, from Virginia to Cape Cod. One of them, "*Cocktails at the White House*," depicting a gathering of all the Presidents and First Ladies, hangs in the executive mansion. He is represented by the family-owned Anchor & Palette Gallery in Bay Head, New Jersey, where the artist resides as well. A website of his work is located at www.dicklabonte.com.

Jane Law of Surf City on Long Beach Island, New Jersey, is celebrating twenty-five years in her own studio-gallery on the island. Prior, while living in Westfield, New Jersey, Jane received her M. A. from New York University and assisted in class there. She also earned a graduate degree at Ohio State University and a B. A. from Otterbein College in Ohio (her home state). She was an assistant professor of art at Union College in New Jersey. Jane won various Woman Of The Year Awards from Long Beach Island, Ocean County, and New Jersey, and is in *Who's Who Of American Women*, N. J. *And East*. Her paintings were featured in *American Artist* and *Color Publications*. She is a member of PWCS and GSWS.

Joyce Lawrence has been painting and drawing since early childhood. Her talent matured as she studied fine art at Stockton State College in New Jersey and The Pennsylvania Academy Of Fine Arts. Her work has won many awards at juried shows and is found in collections and prestigious galleries throughout the United States and Europe. Many of her paintings may be seen in the form of book covers, greeting cards, illustrations, corporate and advertising art, and limited edition prints. Specializing in oil painting and pastels, Joyce describes her style as "contemporary realism with a touch of nostalgia." Still lifes, portraits, and landscapes of the Jersey Shore are some of her favorite subjects. She is a lifelong resident of Tuckerton, New Jersey, where she paints and sells her work from her Bay Moon Art Studio. A website of her work is located at www.tuckerton.com.

Robert A. Loder Jr. of Brielle, New Jersey, is a self-taught painter and has won awards at shows throughout New Jersey. His acrylic paintings on canvas and masonite, as well as his pen and ink sketches and photography, concentrate on the New Jersey shore, Maine, Chesapeake Bay, and Cape Cod. His paintings appear in private collections in the United States and Europe. He is a member of the American Artists Professional League, the Cape May County Art League, the Westfield Art Association, the Ocean County Artists Guild, the Manasquan River Group Of Artists, and the Laurelton Art Society. Robert is a graduate of the University of Pennsylvania where he studied journalism. He has been a newspaper reporter and editor, and a public relations and marketing executive in the healthcare field. His wife, Shirley, manages their gallery, Gull Studios, in Bay Head, New Jersey.

Susan Walsh McLean studied art at Caldwell College but did not begin painting seriously until her children were grown and she retired from teaching English. In the tradition of Jersey Shore impressionism, Susan uses a variety of styles. "The Beach House" series, seen at Thistledown Gallery in Spring Lake, New Jersey, shows this eclecticism. Her paintings have been exhibited at Lincoln Center and hang in private and corporate collections in several states. A past president of the Manasquan River Group Of Artists, Susan is a member of the Guild Of Creative Art in Shrewsbury, New Jersey, the Ocean County Art Guild, and the Art League Of The Sandhills in North Carolina. Her website is www.geocities.com/susan005.

Pauline Mickle grew up in Northumberland, England, where she developed her love of painting by sketching the beautiful countryside. She has lived in the United States since 1947. Pauline prefers watercolor, as it is easier to use for outdoor painting. She likes to paint on location whenever possible, and her favorite subjects are landscapes, beach scenes, flowers, and trees. She has studied with Earl Tyler, Pat Lafferty, and Lucile Geiser, and is a member of the Manasquan River Group of Artists and Ocean County Artists' Guild, where she teaches watercolor. She demonstrates for various local groups and displays her work at many outdoor shows.

Sheila Mickle, an artist and art teacher, is a native of the Point Pleasant area in New Jersey. She is a graduate of Millersville University in Pennsylvania and teaches art at Point Pleasant Borough High School. Sheila specializes in pen and ink drawings and calligraphy, but also works in acrylics, watercolors, and mixed media. Her work has been displayed in local and regional juried art exhibitions, as well as many retail outlets. Her drawings and calligraphy have been featured in COAST *Magazine*, Notecards of the Jersey Shore, cookbooks, calendars, brochures, and several local history books.

Patty Niebling has lived in the Bay Head, New Jersey area all her life. She attended Sweet Briar College and Parsons School Of Design in New York, where she studied commercial and fashion illustration. She has continued to take specialized courses in drawing, computer graphic design, and pastels. Her subject matter includes Barnegat Bay, beach scenes, still life, portraiture, life at the stable, decorative wall design and murals, and more. Patty won second prize at the Monmouth Art Alliance Riverview Hospital Show, second prize at the Paper Mill Playhouse Show in Millburn, New Jersey, and exhibited at The Annual Pastel Society Of America Show in New York. She has been a member of the Ocean County Artists' Guild in Island Heights. Her work can be seen in New Jersey at Anchor & Palette Gallery in Bay Head, Main Street Gallery in Manasquan, and Thistledown Gallery in Spring Lake.

Sue T. Oliver is a native of New Jersey. She grew up in Matawan, and now lives in Ocean. She studied art education at Glassboro State College (now Rowan College) in New Jersey and currently teaches art in Avon-By-The-Sea. She developed her fascination for old homes, water, and landscapes in Matawan. Currently residing by the ocean, her specialty has become house portraits, local scenes, and boardwalk scenes. Her style tends toward realism, showing depth and detail with light and shadow; landscaping often features a touch of Impressionism. Her work can be seen at Thistledown Gallery in Spring Lake, New Jersey, and at www.thistledowngallery.com.

Virginia Perle has been painting and drawing since early childhood. She went on to study Fine Arts at Montclair State College in New Jersey and with renowned watercolor artists as well. She has exhibited extensively throughout the northeast, especially in New York and Pennsylvania. Her paintings can be found in private and corporate collections, a United States congressional office, and twenty-nine foreign countries. She recently exhibited some of her work in the rotunda of the House Of Representatives office building in Washington, D. C., and at the Statehouse in Trenton in a summer-long, single-artist exhibit. Her watercolors cover a wide range of subjects including landscapes, seascapes, city scenes, still lifes, and portraits. Virginia resides in Toms River, New Jersey.

Patricia Rainey is represented by galleries and private collections throughout New England, the metropolitan New York area, and New Jersey. Basically self-taught, her love of the landscape and rugged coastline of New England is reflected in her realistic oil and watercolor paintings. The quaintness and character of the rural areas as well as the many villages along the coastline are the focal points of most of her latest works. Patricia's work can be viewed at www.PatriciaRaineyStudios.com.

Greg Rogers is a self-taught artist, painting mostly in watercolor. His primary subjects are scenes at the Jersey Shore of both present and by-gone days. As a lifetime resident of Point Pleasant, New Jersey, with roots going back five generations, he enjoys capturing moments reflecting those things that have always made it a pleasant place to live: the serenity of an evening boat ride, the beauty of local wildlife, and the romanticism of those that make their living at sea. Greg is a professional software engineer and a published author. He is married with four children. Greg's paintings are available at Bridge Pointe Gallery in Point Pleasant.

Muriel Rogers' paintings reflect her passion for color—particularly the colors found in nature. She is widely recognized for her masterly blending and mingling of pigment to capture the fleeting effects of light and atmosphere. Her work, rendered in a combined realistic-impressionistic style, often focuses on the ever-changing colors of the sky. Muriel developed her painting technique through many years of private instruction and workshops led by nationally known artists. She is a prolific painter, and her work is collected nationally and has been featured on cable TV and in the watercolor magazine, *American Artist*. Muriel is a New Jersey native and graduate of Georgian Court College. She is represented by Anchor & Palette Gallery in Bay Head, New Jersey. Muriel's studio is in her home in Colts Neck, New Jersey.

Nicholas P. Santoleri, a nationally known artist, is acclaimed for the rich detail and realistic style of his watercolors. Nick splits his time between his homes in Pennsylvania and Cape May, New Jersey. The classic Victorian buildings and the natural beauty of the seaside inspired Nick's Cape May collection of artwork. Recognized for his paintings of Philadelphia area landmarks (including Independence Hall, Valley Forge, and Boathouse Row), Nick says his inspiration has come from many areas up and down the East Coast. His artwork that appears in this book, and other limited edition prints, is available at over five hundred galleries across the United States and Canada and on his websites at www.Artist1.com and www.CapeMayArt.com.

Elaine Sgambati began her study of painting at the Ridgewood Art Institute in 1965. She furthered her studies at the Art Students League Of New York and exhibited widely in that area, winning many prestigious awards. After teaching for fourteen years at the Ridgewood Art Institute and nine years at the Ocean County Artists' Guild, Elaine fulfilled her dream of owning her own art school and gallery in 1995 when Riverview Art School And Gallery was opened in Island Heights, New Jersey. The school and gallery are located in an 1880 Victorian farmhouse that has been transformed into one of the most respected art centers in New Jersey, with a staff of seven instructors offering year-round art classes for adults and children, as well as special summer programs. Elaine's work includes portrait, still life, floral, landscape, and figurative. She is represented by S. Morantz Galleries in Cliffside Park, New Jersey, and other fine galleries in the tri-state area. Her artwork can be viewed at www.eSgambati.com.

Ludlow Thorston describes himself as a "truly American watercolorist," a man whose technique and individual interpretation reflect sincerity and dedication to his art. His medium is aquarelle, a transparent technique in which the white of the paper is used for light. Bold strokes, washes, and subtle dashes of color are added to produce fresh, vibrant paintings. Ludlow Thorston is a member and past president of the New Jersey Watercolor Society. A graduate of Newark School Of Fine Art in New Jersey and New York University, he is recognized as a major talent in the medium of watercolor painting. Ludlow and his wife, Nell, reside in Island Heights, New Jersey, where his gallery is located.

Margaret Tourison Berndt travels the globe gathering reference material for paintings of unique and interesting boats indigenous to specific areas. Experiencing the moment and depicting her personal vision has become a signature element in her work and brought her acclaim as the only fine artist allowed access by the America^3 Foundation to depict the first all-women team to vie for the prestigious America's Cup. It is that same spirit which has taken her to a small island in the San Blas region of the Caribbean, where she lived in a thatched hut among the Kuna Indians studying their watercraft. A published artist, Margaret has work hanging in many corporate, municipal, and private collections. She has a line of note cards available through museum shops and fine gift stores. A website of her work is located at www.tillerandtide.com. Margaret has summered at the Jersey Shore since she was a child and currently resides in Grand Haven, Michigan.

Theresa Troise Heidel's watercolors, painted primarily on location, reflect a love of architecture and keen understanding of light and atmosphere. She is a graduate of St. Peter's College in Jersey City, New Jersey, and undertook post-graduate studies at the Accademia delle Belle Arti in Florence, Italy. She also studied under Ferdinand Petrie at the Ridgewood Art Institute in Ridgewood, New Jersey, where she later taught watercolor painting. Theresa's paintings have been featured in *Jersey Shore Vacation Magazine*, *The Jersey Shore Guide Book*, *Jersey Shore Home & Garden*, *Eclectic Magazine*, and on the cover of the 1995 *Monmouth County Cancer Society Ad Book Journal*, as well as in advertisements for the Monmouth County Tourism Board. Her watercolors have also been featured in *American Artist* magazine (December, 1989). Theresa is represented by Oceanside Gallery in Belmar, New Jersey, and Carol Bancroft and Friends in Bethel, Connecticut. She resides in Ridgefield Park, New Jersey.

Lea Colie Wight grew up in the Philadelphia area and spent every summer at her grandmother's home by the ocean in Mantoloking, New Jersey. After receiving a B. F. A. from The Minneapolis College Of Art And Design, she eventually returned to the Jersey Shore, opening Main Street Gallery in Manasquan over twenty years ago. Thanks to a supportive family and gallery staff, Lea has been able to refocus on her artwork for the past several years. She works primarily in oils, pastels, and etching. Lea resides in Manasquan, New Jersey, with her husband and three children.

Dawn Hotaling "Boys Of Summer"
17" x 28" Watercolor 2000 Collection of Artist Prints Available

Edward J. Kojola "Pals At The Jersey Shore"
8 1/2" x 12" Watercolor 1997
Private Collection Prints Available

Nicholas P. Santoleri
"Dolphin Watchers"
9" x 11 3/4" Pencil 2000
Collection of Artist